Introducing Computing

This timely new text provides an accessible introduction to teaching Computing and computer programming. Specifically designed for non-specialists who need to develop new skills in Computing in order to meet the new curriculum requirements, it offers a useful guide to the subject, alongside worked examples of good practice.

Packed full of practical advice, the book examines different approaches to introducing children from age five to Computing, and describes a wide range of tried and tested projects that have been proven to work in schools. Including case studies and a glossary of key terms, it covers:

- The key concepts in Computing and computational thinking
- Using personal learning networks, social media, and the "wiki curriculum" to develop higher thinking skills and desirable learner characteristics
- Links to the curriculum at Key Stages 1, 2, and 3
- Practical ways to develop children's Computing skills alongside creative writing, art, and music
- Gaming and computer science

Featuring a companion web site, www.literacyfromscratch.org.uk, with extensive support materials, examples of pupils' work, links to software, and downloadable lesson plans, this is an essential text for all teachers and trainees who are responsible for the new Computing curriculum.

Lawrence Williams was for many years an Assistant Head Teacher and Director of Creative Development at an "Outstanding" Science Specialist College in south London. His educational ideas about cross-curricular projects, online teaching and learning, and international collaborations have been widely presented and published, including in ICT textbooks by Routledge. He currently teaches Literacy, ICT, and Computing on Primary and Secondary ITE and MA courses in and around London. He has numerous national and international teaching awards, including the 2012 Naace ICT Impact Award: Life Long Achievement.

Introducing Computing

A guide for teachers

Edited by
Lawrence Williams

Routledge
Taylor & Francis Group

LONDON AND NEW YORK

This book is dedicated to Mary Watson, Janet Croggan, and Susan Williams, for their support over many years.

First published 2015
by Routledge
2 Park Square, Milton Park, Abingdon, Oxon OX14 4RN

and by Routledge
711 Third Avenue, New York, NY 10017

Routledge is an imprint of the Taylor & Francis Group, an informa business

British Library Cataloguing in Publication Data
A catalogue record for this book is available from the British Library

Library of Congress Cataloging in Publication Data
A Catalog record for this book has been requested

ISBN: 978-1-138-02284-3 (hbk)
ISBN: 978-1-138-02285-0 (pbk)
ISBN: 978-1-315-75495-6 (ebk)

Typeset in Helvetica
by Wearset Ltd, Boldon, Tyne and Wear

Contents

Figures

Tables

Contributors

Allison Allen is Director of Outstream Consulting, a Trustee of the Board of Management of Naace, and a Fellow of MirandaNet. She is joint author of Naace's ICT Curriculum Framework, and a consultant for Steljes, having recently completed a consultancy with NfER/Futurelab Enquiring Schools. She is a highly regarded keynote speaker, and offers consultation to UK and international schools and organisations.

Miroslava Černochová graduated from the Faculty of Mathematics and Physics at Charles University, in Prague. She works for the Faculty of Education at Charles University, at the Department of Information Technology and Technical Education. She is responsible for courses focused on ICT applications in teaching and learning as a part of the MA Study Programme for ICT student teachers. From 2003–2006, she was invited to be a member of the Czech Ministry of Education consultative body for the realisation of the Governmental Information Policy in Education (GIPE). Since 2004, she has been chair of the RDC group "IT and Teacher Education" in the ATEE.

Ashlie Cox is a former Brunel PGCE student, and undertook the Literacy from Scratch project for Key Stage 2 during her school practice.

Nic Crowe is Programme Leader for Contemporary Education at Brunel University. His research area is best described as The Fantasy Cultures of Young People. He has a special interest in online games and digital spaces.

Mark Dorling is a primary-trained teacher, with secondary school computer science teaching experience, and is now National CPD Co-ordinator for Computing at School, The Subject Association for Computer Science. His work was a case study that formed part of the evidence in the 2012 Royal Society Report: "Shut Down or Restart?".

Rosie Hussain is a Contemporary Education student at Brunel University. She has recently completed research into teacher attitudes to new technologies.

Nick Mayne teaches Computer Science at the Bishop Ramsey School, in Ruislip Manor, West London, and was instrumental in underpinning the early success of the Literacy from Scratch project.

Francis Naera is a Year 2 teacher at the Swaminarayan School in Neasden, West London, and developed support materials for Literacy from Scratch.

Donna Roberts is a Year 1 teacher at the Swaminarayan School in Neasden, West London, and actively supported the development of teaching materials for Literacy from Scratch.

Lawrence Williams is an experienced classroom practitioner, who currently teaches Literacy, ICT, and Computing on ITE courses at a number of universities in London, and abroad. He is both a Senior MirandaNet Fellow and Ambassador, and has represented "best practice" in the United Kingdom on behalf of the DfES, and for Becta, at international conferences. His interests are in literacy, creative uses of ICT, cross-curricular learning, Computing, and international collaborations, on which he has published widely. He has received many awards, including a National Teaching Award for the "Most Creative use of ICT in Secondary Schools", and the 2012 Naace ICT Impact Award: Life Long Achievement.

Introduction

Lawrence Williams

Following the announcement of the "disapplication" of the ICT Programmes of Study by the Secretary of State for Education at BETT, in
January 2012, teachers at both primary and secondary level have suddenly found themselves needing to acquire a new skill set in Computing,
including computer coding. Following much debate between ICT practitioners (MirandaNet, Naace, and ITTE) and computing experts (CAS and
Computing in Schools), in September 2013 the new Programmes of Study
were published. These are due to be taught in schools from September
2014.

While much of the material in the new Programmes of Study is built on
established skills in ICT and digital literacy (including e-safety), there are
many new elements to be learnt by classroom teachers and -teacher trainees. This book aims to set teachers off on a pathway to success in dealing
with these new skills. It is written by established writers in the ICT world,
by experts in pedagogy, and by experienced practitioners in Computing.

One of the Computing projects described, "Literacy from Scratch", has
an associated web site, on which there are extensive, free, support materials for teachers, together with examples of pupils' work from the ages of
five up to 14. Developed by the editor, Lawrence Williams, the web site
details the progress of a creative approach to computer coding skills,
using the MIT visual programming language, Scratch. The most important
aspect of this web site is that teachers can download completed Scratch

project work by students and by teachers, and they can analyse the actual coding, in a way that other Scratch projects on the web do not allow. Analysing and deconstructing successful coding has been found to be the most efficient way of developing and understanding computer coding.

See: www.literacyfromscratch.org.uk or Google: Literacy from Scratch.

These two support resources therefore need to be studied together:

- "Introducing Computing: A guide for teachers" (Routledge, ed. L. Williams)
- "Literacy from Scratch" web site

We hope that teachers will have sufficient materials to be able to find their way towards providing challenging ways of engaging their pupils to develop Computing skills in a creative way.

Three planning grids to help you to find material relevant to KS1, KS2, and KS3 are given in Tables I.1–I.3.

This introductory book is designed for ICT teachers, and teacher trainees, who need to develop new skills in Computing, in order to meet the requirements of the new Programmes of Study. Projects described cover the age range 5–14 years, and all of them have been successfully trialled in classrooms mainly in West London, and in Prague. This is very much a basic introduction to the teaching of Computing, including the philosophical and pedagogical starting points. No prior knowledge of Computing is assumed.

Getting started in Computing

When we first heard, in the Programmes of Study, that five year olds would need to be able to understand what algorithms are, and to be able to write and debug computer programs, most teachers thought that their world had gone completely mad. However, all of this is neither as improbable, nor as impossible, as it may at first seem. And I say this as an experienced former teacher of English, not as a computer scientist.

One of the suggestions made by the Secretary of State was to use Scratch, a visual programming language, also called a "block-coding" program. I looked at this computer program, which was originally designed at MIT in America for children to use in order to create computer games. I quickly realised that its use could easily be adapted to become the "new PowerPoint", in that it could be used to support the writing of short

Table I.1 Key Stage 1

Programmes of Study

Statutory guidance	Relevant chapter in "Introducing Computing"	Useful URLs
Understand what algorithms are, how they are implemented as programs on digital devices, and that programs execute by following precise and unambiguous instructions	Chapters 2, 3, 4, 5, 6	www.computingatschool.org.uk/primary
Create and debug simple programs	Chapters 3, 4, 5	www.literacyfromscratch.org.uk www.computingatschool.org.uk/primary www.123ict.co.uk/scratch/
Use logical reasoning to predict the behaviour of simple programs	Chapters 3, 4, 5, 6	www.literacyfromscratch.org.uk www.computingatschool.org.uk/primary
Use technology purposefully to create, organise, store, manipulate, and retrieve digital content	Chapters 2, 3, 4, 5, 6	
Recognise common uses of information technology beyond school		www.mirandanet.ac.uk/publications/ict_for_world_peace.htm
Use technology safely and respectfully, keeping personal information private; identify where to go for help and support when they have concerns about content or contact on the internet or other online technologies		www.childnet.com/teachers-and-professionals/back-to-school www.bbc.co.uk/cbbc/topics/stay-safe

Table I.2 Key Stage 2

Programmes of Study		
Statutory guidance	Relevant chapter in "Introducing Computing"	Useful URLs
Design, write and debug programs that accomplish specific goals, including controlling or simulating physical systems; solve problems by decomposing them into smaller parts	Chapters 3, 4, 5	www.literacyfromscratch.org.uk
Use sequence, selection, and repetition in programs; work with variables and various forms of input and output	Chapters 3, 4, 5	www.literacyfromscratch.org.uk
Use logical reasoning to explain how some simple algorithms work and to detect and correct errors in algorithms and programs	Chapters 2, 3, 4, 5	www.literacyfromscratch.org.uk
Understand computer networks, including the internet; how they can provide multiple services, such as the World Wide Web, and the opportunities they offer for communication and collaboration	Chapter 6	www.amazon.co.uk/The-Little-Book-Thunks-Independent/dp/1845900626 www.resources.digitalschoolhouse.org.uk/digital-literacy-a-esafety/105-dsh-online-epassport-primary

Use search technologies effectively, appreciate how results are selected and ranked, and be discerning in evaluating digital content	Chapter 6	Useful video: www.youtube.com/watch?v=bNp4Z P5CDcA&feature=player_embedded Activities www.computingatschool.org.uk/data/uploads/ conf2011/real-life.pdf
Select, use and combine a variety of software (including internet services) on a range of digital devices to design and create a range of programs, systems, and content that accomplish given goals, including collecting, analysing, evaluating, and presenting data and information	Chapters 3, 4, 5	www.mirandanet.ac.uk/resources/
Use technology safely, respectfully and responsibly; recognise acceptable/unacceptable behaviour; identify a range of ways to report concerns about content and contact		www.childnet.com/teachers-and-professionals/ back-to-school

Table I.3 Key Stage 3

Programmes of Study

Statutory guidance	*Relevant chapter in "Introducing Computing"*	*Useful URLs*
Design, use and evaluate computational abstractions that model the state and behaviour of real-world problems and physical systems	Chapter 6	
Understand several key algorithms that reflect computational thinking (for example, ones for sorting and searching); use logical reasoning to compare the utility of alternative algorithms for the same problem	Chapter 6	
Use two or more programming languages, at least one of which is textual, to solve a variety of computational problems; make appropriate use of data structures (for example, lists, tables, or arrays); design and develop modular programs that use procedures or functions	Chapter 2	https://wiki.python.org/moin/BeginnersGuide
Understand simple Boolean logic (for example, AND, OR, and NOT) and some of its uses in circuits and programming; understand how numbers can be represented in binary, and be able to carry out simple operations on binary numbers (for example, binary addition, and conversion between binary and decimal)	Chapter 6	www.literacyfromscratch.org.uk

Understand the hardware and software components that make up computer systems, and how they communicate with one another and with other systems	Chapter 6	
Understand how instructions are stored and executed within a computer system; understand how data of various types (including text, sounds, and pictures) can be represented and manipulated digitally, in the form of binary digits	Chapter 6	
Undertake creative projects that involve selecting, using, and combining multiple applications, preferably across a range of devices, to achieve challenging goals, including collecting and analysing data and meeting the needs of known users		www.mirandanet.ac.uk/resources/
Create, reuse, revise, and repurpose digital artefacts for a given audience, with attention to trustworthiness, design, and usability	Chapters 2, 3, 4, 5, 6	www.mirandanet.ac.uk/resources/
Understand a range of ways to use technology safely, respectfully, responsibly, and securely, including protecting their online identity and privacy; recognise inappropriate content, contact and conduct, and know how to report concerns		www.childnet.com/teachers-and-professionals/back-to-school

stories. I had done this for many years in my own classroom, and have published the idea of writing bi-lingual stories in this way on the World Ecitizens web site.

See: www.worldecitizens.net/projects/curriculum-development/stories-for-children/.

Stories, originally created using the more familiar PowerPoint, and now redeveloped using Scratch, could be illustrated by pupils (as original Art work); they could be animated (actually, much more easily in Scratch than in PowerPoint), and voice-over sound files could also be added, either in English or in a second language. Music could be added as a soundtrack. Suddenly, we had a highly creative, collaborative, and cross-curricular project, as a response to the problem of developing Computing in our schools.

Accordingly, I set out to see to what extent this creative writing project could be developed using Scratch, rather than PowerPoint, and started work with an entire Year 8 cohort in Bishop Ramsey School, Ruislip Manor, in West London. The results of this project are outlined in Chapter 5 of this book, and the Bishop Ramsey pupils' Scratch files are published on the web:

www.literacyfromscratch.org.uk

As a current teacher of primary post-graduate teacher trainees, I also started to teach my university students the whole process of creating stories and other teaching materials, in the same way, and encouraged them to trial this as a Key Stage 2 project on their school practice. This also proved successful, leaving only Key Stage 1 as the final problem area. Happily, trials of the same project, in the Swaminarayan School in Neasden, West London, also proved highly successful, with whole classes of Year 1 and Year 2 pupils successfully meeting all the requirements of the Programmes of Study for Computing at Key Stage 1, in just over a single term's work! The reason for this success is simple: by focusing the work on creative writing, developing stories, drawing backgrounds, creating characters, and animating them, the pupils were eager to find ways to make their stories more exciting, when visually presented. The computer coding came a natural second to them on their working agenda, though a vital aspect of a Computing project, of course!

This book shows how this process developed, but I also thought it necessary to link ideas back to what is now left of the "old" ICT agenda.

This is outlined very effectively in Allison Allen's chapter on "Redefining ICT". We need to keep the best of the old ICT, while developing new Computing courses, and her work, for Naace especially, presents a wealth of ideas based on searching questions asked by teachers, over many years.

Important, also, is the rationale for introducing Computing, aside from any political necessity. As educators, we need to be sure that what we are asking our pupils to do is based on sound pedagogy, and this philosophical foundation is to be found in Miroslava Černochová's chapter: "Philosophy and Computing". Mathematical, scientific, philosophical, and computational thinking are all different, and I believe that we need to equip our students with this full range of thinking skills.

Another requirement in the Programmes of Study is for primary pupils to have an understanding of computer networks. This topic is dealt with by Mark Dorling, who developed a series of lessons for primary pupils while working at the Digital School House, and was one of the contributors to the Royal Society Report which started the whole debate.

There is also a different debate about how to engage pupils in Computing in other ways – for example, by working with computer games. Is this a valid topic for serious study? This argument is presented by a leading expert in gaming, Nic Crowe, and one of his students, Rosie Hussain.

Starting out

Our recommendation is that schools should work out a three-year-build for the development of Computing: it cannot be expected that teachers will suddenly acquire a very new set of teaching skills. After due consideration of the ideas outlined above, and in the subsequent chapters of this book, the starting point should be in using Scratch to develop elementary coding skills, through the Literacy from Scratch approach, starting at Key Stage 1. I know this is possible. While there are obvious CPD issues here, there is a wide range of material available on the web, and this book provides practical advice on where to start, and how to proceed. Other developments, including other programming languages, can be added in the second and third year of the introduction of Computing into our classrooms. We need to see this as an exciting new challenge.

1 Redefining ICT

Allison Allen

Why redefine ICT?

Background

Commissioned by the UK computing community, the Royal Society investigated the subject "ICT" in schools, publishing their "Shut Down or Restart?" report in January 2012. They recommended a rebranding of ICT, with a split of the subject into digital literacy, information technology and computer science, and "Computing" as an umbrella term for the subject as a whole.

The media clamoured that ICT lessons were "boring" – pupils were quoted describing lessons that only taught them how to use Microsoft Office, with a peculiar attention to PowerPoint, possibly perhaps because the National Strategy framework focused more on Office applications rather than the National Curriculum Programme of Study. There were few media reports on the inspirational ICT lessons taking place in many schools.

In the light of the report and the publicised expressions of concern, Michael Gove, the Secretary of State for Education, announced at the 2012 BETT Show that he would "disapply" the old Programme of Study and its attendant attainment targets for ICT from September 2012, allowing schools to develop their own schemes of work, and giving them the opportunity to teach programming and other aspects of computer science.

He announced that ICT was to continue as a National Curriculum subject with a new Programme of Study called "Computing" for all maintained schools.

It is worth considering some points from Mr Gove's speech at Bett12:

> Schools, teachers and industry leaders have all told us that the current curriculum is too off-putting, too demotivating, too dull... Instead of children bored out of their minds being taught how to use Word and Excel by bored teachers, we could have 11-year-olds able to write simple 2D computer animations using an MIT tool called Scratch.... By 16, they could have an understanding of formal logic previously covered only in university courses and be writing their own apps for smartphones.

Many ICT teachers were disheartened by these apparently negative comments on the profession. Indeed, simply introducing "Computing" per se will not make a difference, unless we have a meaningful review of both the pedagogy and assessment because these affect pupils' enthusiasm for the subject and their progress in the discipline as well as in technology enhanced learning (TEL). However, within the same speech there were opportunities for technology and computing that went unnoticed, overshadowed by the curricular headlines. Gove's speech continued to reflect and challenge, setting out a vision for UK schools with hints about possible pedagogical change:

> Every day we work in environments which are completely different to those of 25 or 100 years ago.... But there is one notable exception.
>
> Education has barely changed.
>
> The fundamental model of school education is still a teacher talking to a group of pupils. It has barely changed over the centuries... a teacher still stands in front of the class, talking, testing and questioning.
>
> But that model won't be the same in 20 years' time. It may well be extinct in ten.... And the current curriculum cannot prepare British students to work at the very forefront of technological change...
>
> We want a modern education system which exploits the best that technology can offer to schools, teachers and pupils. Where schools use technology in imaginative and effective ways to build the knowledge, understanding and skills that young people need for the future.

> *And where we can adapt to and welcome every new technological advance that comes along to change everything, all over again, in ways we never expected.*

As teachers, we are surrounded by pressure to change our methods and improve our performance. Pressure to perform is rarely so intense and we know we must be able to demonstrate our pupils' progress – yet teachers set themselves high benchmarks and many have learned to fear failure. Full of self-doubt, it is no surprise that many good teachers are abandoning thorough ICT schemes of work in order to buy or borrow from the rush of untested schemes for the new Computing curriculum. The observant have noted a new trend recently emerged – "Scratch is the new PowerPoint".

However, while there is clearly a change in emphasis, Computing is more than computer science and programming. Good lessons previously taught in ICT will fit the information technology and digital literacy aspects of the Computing curriculum, and schools that have taught the "sequencing instructions" in the old Programme of Study will be able to build on this to address the new computer science content.

Most teachers I meet ask for help "unpicking" the new Computing curriculum. Some resources are emerging with focus on coding and programming and those excellent teachers are beginning to panic, drowning in tense online discussions, apparently new terminology and desperate about the need to learn new skills – from where? Opportunities for new pedagogies, however, are relatively overlooked.

The Ofsted school inspection handbook states that inspectors need to consider how well leaders and managers ensure that the curriculum:

- is broad and balanced (in the context of the school) and meets the needs, aptitudes and interest of pupils
- promotes high levels of achievement and good behaviour and successful progression to the pupils' next stage of education, training or employment
- is effectively planned and taught
- is based at Key Stage 4 on an appropriate balance between academic and vocational courses.

Where any school does not provide the National Curriculum, inspectors will explore the school's reasons; a broad and balanced curriculum is required, including the teaching of ICT. Outstanding teachers regard the National Curriculum Programme of Study (PoS) as a minimum and offer considerable contextually relevant enrichment opportunities. However, if the National Curriculum PoS is viewed as the total of subject learning, then lessons are likely to be deemed inadequate. Ofsted is helpfully clear in describing indicators of outstanding teaching, learning, curriculum, and leadership of ICT. Inadequate achievement is described as follows:

- Pupils' lack of understanding impedes their progress in many aspects of the subject. They develop insufficient skills in using and applying ICT.
- Pupils rarely demonstrate creativity or originality in their use of ICT but seem confined to following instructions.
- Pupils do not work well with others, and do not know how different roles can contribute to successful outcomes when using ICT.
- In secondary schools, significant proportions of students in Key Stage 4 neither study ICT nor develop their skills systematically through other subjects.
- Pupils lack interest and enthusiasm for the subject and cannot describe the relevance of ICT in a technological age.

So the opportunities are twofold: change the curriculum to refresh and focus on computational thinking as well as IT and digital literacy, and change the way we teach our lessons to achieve outstanding teaching and learning. A challenge, but not beyond our reach – we need to focus on understanding the possibilities and revising our existing good practice.

This chapter discusses the "how" – alternative models of pedagogy, approaches to the subject and assessment – to support the "what" (the subject content), and offers some ideas from school case studies, approaches, and conversations. The opportunity for improving the lives and careers of young people and the impact on "UK plc" is compelling.

Changing good ICT lessons into opportunities for new and outstanding learning

Change will not come if we wait for some other person or some other time. We are the ones we've been waiting for. We are the change that we seek.

(Barack Obama)

The change of curriculum with its promise of greater freedom to schools is a terrific opportunity to review and adapt ICT schemes of work. It is adamantly *not* necessary to abandon good lessons designed to deliver the old ICT curriculum, but teachers do need to consider how learning outcomes might be more effectively achieved and what needs to be done to ensure they deliver the outcomes of the new Computing curriculum. Inevitably some lessons will not carry over, but the reality is that if a lesson worked well for the old curriculum, with a tweak here and there it will work for the new! I have included examples of approaches; although they are from all kinds of curriculum areas, all are relevant to teaching the Computing curriculum as well as supporting cross-curricular safe and creative use.

While your main reference will be the new Computing curriculum online publication, it is worth also considering some of the good-quality guidance that has been produced by organisations such as Naace and Computing At School (CAS), including:

- "Naace Curriculum Framework" for Key Stages 1–3 with further resources including Assessment and CPD freely available here: www.naace.co.uk/naacecurriculum and www.naace.co.uk/curriculum
- "Computer Science: A Curriculum for Schools" produced by CAS, describes what a Computing curriculum at school might look like: www.computingatschool.org.uk/index.php?id=cacfs. More resources are available from www.computingatschool.org.uk/and the CAS Community
- "Computing 2014 – Guidance for Primary Teachers" published by CAS and written in collaboration by CAS and Naace members. The guide has been sent to schools: www.naace.co.uk/curriculum/primaryguide. The guidance is also relevant to KS3.

We are affected one way or another in our daily lives by the activities represented in curricular subjects and few more so than Computing. Much of the time, ICT infrastructure is so embedded as to be invisible and our interface with it seamless, yet we marvel at "Smart" technologies and devices that allow us to do things we would never have dreamt possible, while relying on ubiquitous ICT to allow us to engage with daily activities. The ICT report from the Forum for the Future, *Connect, Collaborate, Change* (www.forumforthefuture.org/project/connect-collaborate-change/overview), featured in the *Guardian* in February 2012, shows that one of the greatest areas of potential is for ICT to create new behaviours or systems and considers where ICT can achieve the biggest sustainability gains by enabling system change.

Computing and ICT thus must develop as an essential part of the school curriculum so that our learners, who will ultimately be our leaders and agents for change, understand it and are enabled to design tools for action as well as a stimulus for fresh thinking about where interventions can successfully be made. Computing and ICT could be the most powerful enablers of transformation we possess; with excellent teaching and intelligent use of the curriculum, our pupils have the ability to support the change needed by taking good ideas to a scale that fundamentally alters the way we live. We need to address not only the "what" of Computing, but "how" we are teaching it.

> In cross-curricular use, a new approach to teaching Maths at KS3 is exemplified by Cornerstone Maths with use of convergent technologies that bring together computing and technology-enhanced learning – exploiting innovative use of digital technology for learning mathematics. In this way, abstraction is removed so that pupils enjoy learning hard-to-grasp mathematical concepts, such as average velocity. Research shows that a combination of teacher professional development and digital mathematics materials improve student mathematics learning and may lead to systemic change in the professional development of teachers of mathematics.
>
> http://tinyurl.com/cornerstonemaths

There are so many questions – mobile learning, for example: How do we prepare for "Learning in the moment, learning across space and learning across time"? (Naomi Norman) or "...just in time, just enough and just for me" (John Traxler)? How do we reap the benefits of mobile apps and their creation without the risks? How can we ensure coding delivers the learning outcomes pupils need? How do we develop the learner who enjoys the challenge of a "smorgasbord of e-learning"? Can we develop the use of ethical hacking, "Hacking to Learn"? How do we use social (vicarious) learning? What about the opportunity afforded by the "flipped classroom"? Should our pupils be aware of the way 3D printing will affect them in the future? How does understanding the history and evolution of the computer increase our understanding of our digital future?

Taking advantage of collaborative technology tools to develop higher thinking skills and desirable learner characteristics

Online learning is often designed around "walled gardens" so that learner safety is prioritised. However, this often means that it is a push model – an online version of the teacher-led classroom. Today, technology has developed so that safety and security are easier to achieve. The rise of social media, proliferation of mobile devices, and the blend of technologies affords us the benefits of "Connected learning" – such as the boy who learned to play the saxophone with the help of a stranger across the world via YouTube.

In his controversial book *Deschooling Society* (HarperCollins, 1971), Ivan Illich anticipates "learning webs" where people learn from each other through advanced technology and communications.

> *The operation of a peer-matching network would be simple. The user would identify himself by name and address and describe the activity for which he sought a peer. A computer would send him back the names and addresses of all those who had inserted the same description. It is amazing that such a simple utility has never been used on a broad scale for publicly valued activity.*
>
> *(Ivan Illich)*

Illich's hypothesis was echoed in 1999 by Professor Sugata Mitra's "Hole in the Wall" experiments provocatively focusing on unsupervised learning and computers (www.hole-in-the-wall.com). Mitra observed:

> *The Hole in the Wall experiments were first implemented in 1999, when a computer with an internet connection was embedded into a wall, for children to discover and use unsupervised. The wall adjoined a slum; and only a month later, it was evident that the children had taught themselves to use the computer and also picked up some skills in English and Mathematics ... groups of children ... given free and public access to computers and the Internet can:*
>
> 1. *Become computer literate on their own, that is, they can learn to use computers and the Internet for most of the tasks done by lay users.*

2. *Teach themselves enough English to use email, chat and search engines.*
3. *Learn to search the Internet for answers to questions in a few months' time.*
4. *Improve their English pronunciation on their own.*
5. *Improve their mathematics and science scores in school.*
6. *Answer examination questions several years ahead of time.*
7. *Change their social interaction skills and value systems.*
8. *Form independent opinions and detect indoctrination.*

(Source document: http://tinyurl.com/pdh4lqq)

So, what are the implications for learners? What skills do they need to take advantage of learning through social media? What behaviours do we need to encourage and model ourselves?

Digital literacy

Digital literacy is a key part of the Computing curriculum and embodies the essential skills that support new ways of learning. There are multiple definitions of digital literacy. The version I prefer and which Naace adopts is:

"Digital literacy involves critically engaging with technology and developing a social awareness of how a number of factors including commercial agendas and cultural understandings can shape the ways in which technology is used to convey information and meaning.

It means being able to communicate and represent knowledge in different contexts and to different audiences (for example, in visual, audio, or textual modes). This involves finding and selecting relevant information, critically evaluating and re-contextualising knowledge and is underpinned by an understanding of the cultural and social contexts in which this takes place.

Digital literacy gives young people the ability to take advantage of the wealth of new and emerging opportunities associated with digital technologies whilst also remaining alert to the various challenges technology can present. In short, digital literacy is the 'savviness' that allows young people to participate meaningfully and safely as digital technology becomes ever more pervasive in society."

(Handbook: "Digital literacy across the curriculum", C. Hague and S. Payton, Futurelab, 2010)

This definition of digital literacy strongly correlates with Guy Caxton and Howard Rheingold's articulations on the literacies needed for self-organised learning.

Literacies for self-organised learning

Guy Claxton's characteristics of a confident explorer/researcher	Howard Rheingold's social media literacies
● Curiosity, inquisitiveness, attentiveness (to an odd result, faint pattern)	● Attention: knowing how to focus and how to divide your attention without losing focus
● The ability to be a good source-tester; scepticism	● Critical consumption ("rubbish detection")
● Determined and observant, maintain focus; the pleasure of being rapt	● Participation, particularly the more constructive modes of participation that are useful to others
● Patience: ability to tolerate confusion and "hang out in the fog", don't rush to closure	● Collaboration: being ready to organise together, and enable a collective response to emerge
● Knowing how to be experimental, including "tinkering", creating drafts and hands-on construction	● Network awareness: the hybrid connection of reputation, social capital, presentation of self and other sensitivity to individual positioning within the collective
● Imaginative, good relationship with own intuition	
● Collaborative and independent	
● Degree of self-awareness and reflectiveness	

(Adapted from: David Jennings, http://alchemi.co.uk/archives/ele/agile_learning.html)

However, my caveat is that neither Claxton nor Rheingold refers to e-safety; being confident about technology does not necessarily equate to competence, especially "higher level" critical thinking skills. Staying safe online requires the ability to make appropriate and informed decisions. The Byron Review refers to the need to increase children's resilience to harmful and inappropriate material but this does mean that, as traditional literacy is essential for all subjects, so digital literacy needs to be incorporated into all teaching. Every teacher can offer a different perspective as to how technology can add value in their subject.

Personal learning networks

If we follow Sugata Mitra's observations and the consensus on the need for digital and learning literacies, our pupils then need support to adopt these literacies, if they are to take advantage of the affordances of technology supported networks.

The increasingly complex relationships that are emerging in support of learning frequently involve a personal learning network (PLN). The idea is not new – learners create connections and develop a network that contributes to their learning development and knowledge (see Figure 1.1). The learner does not have to know these people personally or ever meet them in person.

However, some teachers do not welcome students' out-of-school knowledge entering the classroom and, indeed, feel threatened by it. One secondary deputy head teacher commented, "They (pupils) know more than we do about ICT. They're learning it off the internet; they're learning it off each other and we're trying to stamp it out!" They would not be persuaded that this self-organised learning was good and could be channelled for the benefit of pupils and the school.

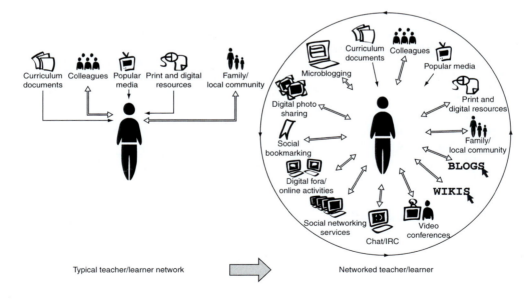

Figure 1.1 Twenty-first century shift to personal learning networks (PLNs). (Graphics adapted from Alex Couros, licensed under CC/ATT/NC.)

Bringing in self-organised learning into the classroom can be seen as undermining teachers' authority when it is framed as a challenge, but for other teachers it leads to a celebration of self-organised learning, sometimes leading to the role of teacher-pupil-learner changing according to context. One primary school teacher consistently assessed a year 6 pupil as "NC level 4" because "That's all we have to assess to in primary". In conversation with the girl and other pupils, I found that she had designed, constructed, and was managing her own web site – it was so informative and accessible that other children visited it regularly and recommended it to friends outside of the school. The teacher subsequently celebrated the skills and thinking involved, assessing the pupil at a more appropriate level and supporting her to become an ICT mentor to other pupils and teachers.

Points to consider: How can we capture and celebrate what our pupils have learned – how do we even know such learning has occurred? And if we don't know – how can we assess it? What is the role of the teacher – the sage, facilitator or something different?

Part of the concept of PLNs is the familiar theory of connectivism developed by George Siemens and Stephen Downes – a perspective similar to Vygotsky's "zone of proximal development", explaining the difference between what a learner can do without help and what he or she can do with help. (In the zone of proximal development, students cannot complete tasks unaided, but can complete them with guidance.)

If we add "technology" to the mix of connections and networks that contribute to PLNs, the learning can appear to us more daunting and complex even while we acknowledge how learners are empowered.

Most learning needs today are becoming too complex to be addressed in "our heads". We need to rely on a network of people (and, increasingly, technology) to store, access, and retrieve knowledge and motivate its use. This is critical today; the rapid development of knowledge means that we need to find new ways of learning and staying current. We must begin to conceive learning as socially networked and enhanced by technology – a symbiosis of people and technology forming our learning networks.

We rely on Google, libraries, friends, social bookmarks/tags, etc. to serve as our personal learning network (and store the knowledge external to ourselves). When we need something, we go to our network (know-where is more important than know-how or know-what) … or we expand our network. In the end, the constant act of connecting in order to stay current is a much more reflective model of learning than constructivism (Siemens).

Communities of Practice and Communities of Learning are more structured examples of shared interest group learning. MOOCs (Massive Open Online Courses) are an extreme version of these; typically courses are free to unlimited numbers of geographically diverse participants but tend to use the classroom "push" model. Cambridge GCSE Computing Online is a timely example of a MOOC. The lack of teacher time available to students studying on a MOOC, however, has highlighted the value of using peer assessments and peer appraisal as an integral part of the learning design of a MOOC (Guardia *et al.*, 2013).

Social media, backchannels

The ways in which social media can be used to engage parents in their children's learning have been a topic of discussion in many schools I visit. Many ICT Mark schools have found that it can be easier to reach parents through the online tools they use already, rather than trying to encourage them to visit the school's web site, and it is certainly more effective and efficient than paper. Although many schools use text messaging as a means of communication to parents regarding an individual child's attendance, progress, and so on, the possibility of providing timely information on the topics being taught is seen as an exciting way of encouraging parents to support their child's learning at home. There are valued opportunities for the school to promote itself within its community and for teachers to share practice.

In some ICT Mark schools (www.naace.co.uk/ictmark) and several 3rd Millennium Learning Award schools (www.naace.co.uk/thirdmillennium-learningaward), social media offers the potential to engage children in learning, encourage collaboration, and develop questioning and reflection skills through, for example, blogging.

Ideas from school case studies:

A. A teacher who asked groups of children to role play the characters in the Shakespeare play they were studying on a blogging site.
B. A secondary school teacher who struggled to engage girls in literature and found that, through setting up a teacher-controlled multi-access Twitter account, enthusiastic pupils contributed book reviews and discussions, the idea spreading through more resistant pupils until the Twitter feed received 200 pupil comments in two weeks after school and in lessons. The Twitter feed displayed on the class whiteboard became an effective classroom backchannel and source of productive debate, as well as a permanent record of contributions.

Backchannel communication is a secondary electronic conversation that takes place at the same time as a lesson. On an informal basis, this might involve students using a chat tool or Twitter to discuss a lesson as it is happening. Sometimes, like the school mentioned above, these background conversations are brought into the foreground as a formal part of lesson interaction as the teacher encourages pupils to join in with questions or comments, sharing their feedback with one another without disrupting the lesson flow.

When teachers integrate questions or comments from the backchannel into their lessons, or when pupils, emboldened by positive feedback, broach questions they might otherwise leave unasked, the backchannel can help guide the lesson. Whether the backchannel exists as a spontaneous chat among a few pupils or displayed as text on a board, the attraction is its immediacy as a real-time conversation in parallel with the traditional lesson. The method is not appropriate for all school contexts and can be distracting – however, a collaborative mindmap (there are several free and pay-for tools) can be a good alternative, while developing deep thinking and a way to collaborate that appeals to diffident pupils.

Most of these innovative schools are well aware of the potential dangers of social networking for young people, such as cyberbullying, inappropriate contact, or spending too much time on social networks. They stress the need for clear policies that are developed with pupils and communicated to parents, along with whole-school responsibility for education about online behaviour as well as monitoring and modelling safe activity. Typically, these technology-savvy schools also seek to bridge the digital divide and achieve equity of home access.

Ideas from school case studies:

Case study A

In one primary school study (not published), an activity was set up to encourage children to seek and offer peer support in an online problem-solving task using MSLogo. Because the school had concerns about using Twitter in unsafe home environments, the activity used synchronous discussion on the school's learning platform. The activity resulted in creative, confident use of MSLogo to solve problems and highly improved questioning/answering skills. Computational thinking emerged through focused dialogue.

Case study B

Another primary school described in its ICT Mark assessment visit (not published), how they set up a "homework" discussion forum on its learning platform and found in an annual survey that pupil enjoyment of homework went up from 60 per cent to 90 per cent; in addition it enabled staff to discover and deal appropriately with a confidence issue for a new pupil. Teachers were asked about work–life balance regarding this use of forums; one answered, "The children know we have a life outside school. If I'm not online when they want help, another pupil jumps in and helps." The pupils confirmed that this approach worked well and made them feel confident.

It is clear that these schools are confident that the potential risks can be addressed, while recognising the need for schools to take a measured approach, learning from evidence how to maximise the opportunities and prepare young people to engage productively and confidently online.

At Bett13, Ann S. Michaelsen (a Norwegian teacher) made an inspiring presentation about her project on using social media to connect educators, students, and experts worldwide. She described the project brief:

"Participants will be shown how to use social media like Skype, YouTube, blogs and Twitter to get in contact with students and teachers from other parts of the world. Students communicate and learn from peers in the outside world using social media and teachers introduce new material to the students on personal blogs using authentic material like videos from YouTube and TED. Curriculum goals are the basis for learning, not textbooks, and students find how different topics can be used to cover the curriculum goals. Questions and challenges are set by the students with help from teachers. Students offer feedback to fellow students. The goal is self-paced differentiated learning where every student can progress individually and the teacher can keep track of this. We explore how it is possible to use digital age learning in an authentic real-world practice, modelling real-world problems."

David Mitchell introduced Quadblogging into his primary school with truly startling success (http://quadblogging.net/). It is a way of getting pupils involved in writing and responding to writing by others around the world; the focus topics of the blogs vary widely.

"Imagine four schools that had a partnership/agreement that would mean that for a four week cycle, each school's blog would be the focus for one week out of four. Each school in the Quad would spend some time visiting the blog of the school for that week, leave comments, etc. . . .

What many people don't know is the pedagogy behind the good practice that goes into the learning behind a great blog. . . . Firstly, a blog is an outcome, this outcome has seen many stages before it is made public. And in the public nature of the outcome lies the magic of the engagement that so many teachers that use blogging preach about. . . . We ask our learners to consider their audience daily or weekly. What's the point when they are writing for their teacher alone? From my experience the learner also knows what we will be writing in their books for developmental points too. Give a learner a global platform to publish their learning and you'll see these learners apply 100% effort because if they don't, their audience will tell them! . . . At another level blogging is so important in education because of the community that surrounds it – a generous group of sharing learners all at different levels of their learning journeys. Comments from other learners are more powerful than any other comments. Over the last 12 months, my learners have received over 8,000 comments. These 8,000 comments are sometimes 300–400 words long with links to examples and suggestions too. How powerful is that? More powerful than my 3 stars and a wish? My learners think so!"

Wiki curriculum

There would seem to be parallels between the social media and blogging models described above and the "wiki" approach to designing the curriculum that would allow teachers and experts to collaborate in tailoring lessons for schools proposed by Michael Gove during his speech at Bett12:

> I believe the dispersed wisdom of the best teachers in this country and globally will be better than any bureaucracy's attempts to freeze

*in time and for all time the best way of teaching ... technology could be used to develop the content – and a **wiki approach** could be taken to developing new curriculum materials..., this will allow teachers to cover "innovative, specialist and challenging" topics.*

For many teachers, this poses a real test: used to a fully described PoS and attendant attainment targets with schemes of work delivered by National Strategies, moving to teaching the new PoS as a baseline with absolute freedom as to "how" is a difficult change. In an environment where schools are encouraged to be competitive via league tables, the notion of sharing such a development is disturbing. A helpful simplification is:

The most important aspect of such a self-governed curriculum is in "tweaking" what the government provided in previous years, but with the new ability to "change it and adapt it". So we have something which I think is a little more relevant and agile.... So, for instance, take Naace's ICT framework, and take the bits of that that appeal to you.

(Miles Berry, Past Naace Chair)

Or put even more simply: "Teachers learning from each other" (Bob Geldof:MirandaNet/BETT13).

A wiki differs from a blog because the content is created without any defined owner and little inherent structure, allowing it to emerge according to the needs of the users.

High editorial standards in medicine have led to the idea of expert-moderated wikis. Medicine is ahead of education with its use of software which supports mapping professional knowledge, known as Medical Subject Heading or MESH. In education, MESH, the **M**apping **E**ducational **S**pecialist KnowHow initiative, is a project that borrows the idea from medicine. MESH Guides are created to provide teachers and other educators with quick access to summaries of research-based specialist knowledge to support their professional judgment. (www.meshguides.org).

Governments think the way to improve learning outcomes is to change the curriculum. What this does is make teachers spend their precious time changing teaching plans and documentation rather than focusing on improving the learning of every child. MESH provides support for teachers in making decisions about learning approaches and shows policy makers what can be done to make a difference to each child's learning.

(Margaret Shirley, primary teacher, Rural Australia)

Because of the nature of a wiki curriculum, there are issues of validation – peer and expert/co-validation The observations that David Mitchell makes about "comments from other learners" are equally applicable to the notion of a "wiki curriculum"; "participants are accredited by members of the wiki community, who have a vested interest in preserving the quality of the work product, on the basis of their ongoing participation" – the idea of validation through peer and expert collaboration becomes easier to understand.

Interestingly, MESH could be used by learners as part of a PLN or "Flipped Classroom":

As a young person I recall a dreadful week when the teacher was teaching fractions. I had clearly missed some vital explanation and no idea what the teacher was talking about. I was lucky in that my parents helped me out. Having a resource like MESH which is linked with different teachers' explanations and different approaches to a topic gives children the chance to go over work they can't understand in their own time.

(Anonymous, CEO, Australian internet-based company)

Agile learning, informative assessment, and the Computing agenda

As teachers, some of our best and most memorable lessons are those where the "learning journey" takes an unexpected turn because of pupils' questions, contributions, and unforeseen problems. One of the great opportunities of the new, more flexible curriculum, with its lack of attainment targets, is the chance to change what and how we teach.

Teachers on a recent Naace PDE Computing course expressed surprise that "computational thinking" was being observed in school as a transferable way of solving problems and exploring situations – pupils had visibly changed their approach to problem solving, and said it was because of Computing lessons and the algorithmic methods they had used. Other teachers had taken advantage of this new problem-solving approach and were varying their teaching – a demonstration of agile learning.

Agile learning is a proven approach to learning that is particularly relevant to Computing. A useful definition is that of an approach to self-managed collaborative learning that combines maximum flexibility with reduced cost by using freely available online tools and resources; it is, if you like, the dynamic planning of learner activities. A knowledge-building community or a community of learning are good examples of agile learning. Agile learning also can refer to supporting individual learning paths – for example, how students progress through a set of learning outcomes in traditional e-learning becomes "giving students what they need as needed".

In addition, many schools are developing agile learning spaces that are not just about flexibility, but also about the ability for easy and quick configuration changes to suit the learning need at the time. The popularity of mobile devices has enhanced the potential for "just-in-time" resources.

We can make sense of this by taking reference from computing development methods and applying them to learning;

> *Agile learning can be described as adaptive where learning milestones are identified but there is flexibility in the path to reach them, and sometimes the realities and milestones change. It is learner-centric, focusing on individuals and interactions, getting resources that work, collaboration and responding to change – an iterative process*
>
> *Traditional learning, by contrast, is predictive based on analysing abilities and planning in detail with risks known. It is teacher-centric but in some schools, teachers can describe exactly what is planned for the entire length of a course, but if something goes wrong, they may have difficulty changing direction.*

Points to consider: have online tools and resources sufficient potential that you could create a social learning experience delivering what your learners want and need? If so, agile learning may be easier than you think because the approach is quick and responsive, and keeps learners engaged. It fits your timescale, learning preferences, and outcomes you need, enabling you to change things as you go along, while avoiding any "institutional inertia".

An approach to classroom scenarios

My classroom looks, feels, and sounds most of the time like a busy office. Pupils are allowed to get up and ask for help or offer advice freely – as long as the activity is purposeful and supports the learning outcome. By treating young people as adults, they largely behave well and are usually self-policing – I teach in a very mixed catchment, with mixed ability classes.

We often use role play. In one example, we focused on Royal Mail processes; I created groups of four pupils – ability, gender, and nationality mixed. Each group had to discuss with members and decide on who was best for each of four "jobs" – General Manager (targets and final decision), Finance Manager (spreadsheets, controlling spend), Logistics Manager (deciding equipment, where, how much, and/or programming) and Operations Manager (personnel, timing, Gantt). The model required all to work together in various ways.

We started manually sorting addressed envelopes (with a "red herring"), checked by me – lots of fun and frustration! Then the group set up and ran a program dealing with the mail process to get the most efficiency and cost effectiveness. Pupils undertook a whole-group evaluation report ensuring clarity over who did what (this confirmed my assessment). Finally they did a peer and self-assessment (using a professional tool), which was a revelation as each peer assessment gave more praise while identifying difficulties than the self-assessments, which were quite harsh. I have to be quite nimble – support needs vary across lessons. Ofsted, incidentally, loved this approach.

(Head of ICT, secondary school)

Informative assessment

It is important that lessons are not software – or technology – driven but focused on clear teaching and learning objectives where ICT is used as a vehicle to support achievement of those objectives. I am frequently startled by the number of practitioners that do not think about lessons in terms of what learning objectives might be the result: "I wanted them to practise writing"; "I want them to learn Python"; "I don't know why I'm doing it – my teacher said I had to do a poster". Instead, write your lesson and course objectives with the aim of enabling pupils to *demonstrate their ability in the higher levels of thinking as well as subject knowledge.*

Formative assessment is an integral part of teaching and learning. It contributes to learning through providing feedback. It should indicate what is good about a piece of work and why; it should also indicate what is not so good and how the work could be improved. Effective formative feedback will affect what the student and the teacher does next.

Summative assessment demonstrates the extent of a learner's success in meeting the assessment criteria used to gauge the intended learning outcomes of the lesson(s) or project, and contributes to the final mark. It is normally, though not always, used at the end of a unit of teaching. Summative assessment is used to quantify achievement, to reward achievement, and to provide data for selection, the next stage in education or employment.

About 25 years ago, I began to realise the need for what I called "informative" assessment that goes beyond "formative" assessment. It is not a top-down approach of teacher perception passed to the learner; it is about sharing and pupil ownership of progress or problems – and it works really well in raising attainment. At the minimum, share the learning outcomes with your pupils – reading them tends to be ignored or received like registration – a necessary chore! Put them on the board, maybe like a spidergram? Link the outcomes to a resource that helps pupils review what they have done – when pupils gain awareness of their own progress, they will be more likely to own the steps to overcome difficulties. Use questioning to develop pupils' self-assessment abilities. Essentially it is all about encouraging effort and actions to improve as a challenge to a "fixed mindset" and to promote metacognition and seeing your pupils as full partners in their success.

Diana Laurillard has argued that learning requires three cycles of communication to occur:

- the teacher must communicate their concepts for the learner to understand;
- the teacher must provide an environment to model the learning and for the learner to practise within;
- the learners must engage in peer communication, providing their own modelling and practice environments to support each other's learning.

The outcomes to which we aspire – in particular, our view of the learner as an active partner – will involve some movement from the teacher-centric or traditional pedagogy to pupil-centric. It is evident that there may be further developments towards adoption of heutagogy (self-determined learning) that will stem from our transformational use of technologies, particularly the mobile technologies.

The concept of heutagogy builds on humanistic theory and approaches to learning described in the 1950s. It is suggested that heutagogy is appropriate to the needs of learners in the twenty-first century, particularly in the development of individual capability.

Assessment is changing from a focus on what teachers do to a focus on what learners do and from product and performance to the processes of learning. Assessment supports learning best when learners understand its function and own the authentic experience (see Figure 1.2).

Although we are "programmed" to learn, it is helpful to receive the right formative feedback, and to be asked what Dylan Wiliam calls "hinge questions" – questions that are based on an important concept that is critical for students to understand; in this respect, "self-organised" learning may fail to offer feedback or formative questions.

The UK Assessment Reform Group (1999) identifies "The big five principles of assessment for learning":

1. The provision of effective feedback to students.
2. The active involvement of students in their own learning.
3. Adjusting teaching to take account of the results of assessment.
4. Recognition of the profound influence assessment has on the motivation and self-esteem of pupils, both of which are critical influences on learning.
5. The need for students to be able to assess themselves and understand how to improve.

The portfolios, projects, and problems emerging from a more agile approach might well count more towards a career in the workplace than school tests and exams.

Michael Gove's disapplication of attainment targets mean that we can look beyond levelling and APP (Assessing Pupils' Progress) to a more granular skills-based approach to assessment, such as badges (visual representations of skill or achievement), reflecting the emphasis on unit testing in agile development and borrowing some of the feedback and goal orientation of video games and applying these to the classroom. Arguably this is a helpful basis for informative feedback, but unless

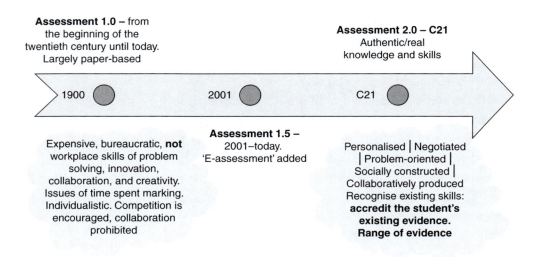

Figure 1.2 Changes to assessment in the twenty-first century.

badges developed as part of a pathway, they are currently skill landmarks.

The heutagogic approach supported by technology means that we have to look much further for evidence of learning (see Figure 1.3).

Although evidence of learning will be in the classroom, it will also be found online – including the school's learning platform, a web site, an e-portfolio, witnessed in a video conference, explicit in a pod cast or blog,

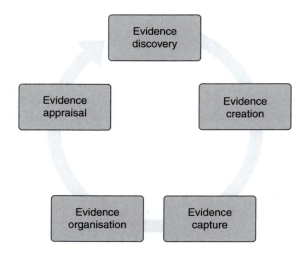

Figure 1.3 Assessment shift: where/what/who?

shared on a forum, and so on. What evidence might look like – printed evidence, web site, questioning, observation, photos, video, pod casting, blog, forum, demonstration; the list is endless and the teacher needs to be imaginative to capture and celebrate evidence of learning and progress. While we ponder the richness of evidence, should we not also consider who might recognise it – the teacher, self, peer, group, remote, crowd.... And once we have the outcome evidence – how to assess and benchmark?

Whatever evidence and/or record of pupils' computing learning is kept, the major consideration is the purpose for keeping or signposting it – individual, class, year, or school portfolios or pupil e-portfolios are useful as reference for many stakeholders, including TAs and temporary teachers who often miss CPD.

Gove believed that the system of "levels" used to report children's attainment and progress was too complicated and made teachers focus too narrowly on skills rather than the broader picture of what a pupil can do. Instead, schools are introducing their own approaches to formative assessment, built into the school curriculum, so that they can check what pupils have learned and whether they are on track to meet expectations at the end of the Key Stage and National Curriculum tests. In practice, it is very difficult to track pupils against national expectations if assessment is based only on local data.

The NfER paper "Primary Assessment and Accountability under the New National Curriculum", October 2013, cautions:

> However, we feel it will be extremely challenging for schools to design new effective assessment frameworks for tracking progress, without external referents, at the same time as they are developing and embedding their approach to teaching the new National Curriculum. There may be an erroneous assumption that teaching the content of the Programmes of Study in the core subjects will ensure pupils are on track to meet the end of Key Stage 2 (KS2) expectations.

There are a number of well-recognised, nationally and locally appropriate frameworks for tracking progress. These include Bloom's taxonomy, ISTE National Educational Technology Standards for Students (NETS*S), Personal, Learning and Thinking Skills (PLTS), Renzulli's Enrichment Triad, Megarrity's Creative Learning Contracts, De Bono's Six Thinking Hats, and so on. The National Curriculum attainment targets, although disapplied, are still applicable to the new Computing curriculum and could be a good baseline or mapping tool; they map easily to Bloom's, for example (see Figure 1.4).

Similarly, a report undertaken by Mick Waters (2007) suggests a move away from detailed level descriptions, and instead emphasis is placed on negotiated key "trajectories" against which students might progress. Robert Fisher offers a relevant comment: "Thinking skills enable pupils to turn their experience into learning. We need to focus on 'knowing how', rather than 'knowing what': learning how to learn" (2005, p. 209).

Bloom's taxonomy divides the way people learn into three domains. One of these is the cognitive domain, which emphasises intellectual out-comes. This domain is further divided into categories. Keywords used and questioning may aid in the establishment and encouragement of critical thinking, especially in the higher levels.

In Computing and ICT activities, pupils should be encouraged to model the systems design (or user-centred design) process, which helps develop higher thinking skills and maps well to Bloom's taxonomy as a means of assessment. This may include designing a digital artefact and using some

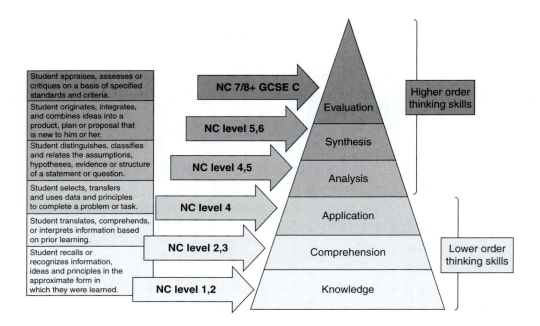

Figure 1.4 Bloom's taxonomy pyramid showing mapping to disapplied ICT attainment levels.

project management ideas – in primary schools as well as secondary. Schools tell us that this works particularly well when the teacher models the process habitually in lessons.

Although some pupils will be able to *write* sufficient evidence to offer obvious evidence of higher thinking skills, many pupils lack the literacy skills to do so, especially in Key Stage 1 and Early Years. Teachers will need to be creative in considering how to gather evidence from younger, EAL or differently abled pupils: questioning (who, how, why, what happened), observation, video, photos, presentation, pupil as teacher, and so on. However, some pupils will demonstrate maturity in thinking and even written articulation prior to transition to KS3 and it will certainly become more evident in KS3 from Year 7 onwards according to pupil ability. A signifier of mature thinking is avoidance of subjective comments, such as "I could of [*sic*] worked quicker".

In a mixed-ability school, typically 10–20 per cent of Year 7 pupils will be able to write an evaluation to support indicative assessment at the highest of Bloom's equivalent to the old NC level 7 or beyond (see Figure 1.5).

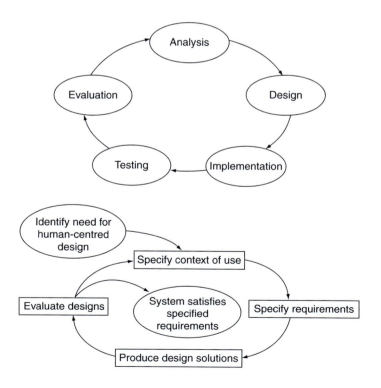

Figure 1.5 Systems design and user-centred design process.

Main stages: Analysis – studying the problem; design – designing a solution; implementation – putting the solution into effect and testing it; evaluation – checking that the solution is working as intended.

In Computing, systems design and user-centred design have considerable overlap. They are central to raising attainment with the Computing curriculum and support development of computational thinking and the Computer Science agenda where appropriate. The principles existed in the old ICT PoS, but are still often neglected, and when I ask children "Who are you doing this for – do you know the audience?", the reply is all too often "No, my teacher said I had to do this".

Both design models allow pupils to access landmarks of higher attainment through developing higher thinking skills. Less able pupils may benefit from encouragement to attempt these tasks and can be determined to "rise to the challenge". All will benefit from understanding what a good evaluation contains and routes to evidence include video, blog, and teacher questioning. It is important that design of digital artefacts is focused on age-appropriate, real projects, such as business, leisure, home, or social contexts with which the pupil can relate; design of mobile apps for a specific task appears successful at both KS2 and KS3, for example.

The American International Society for Technology in Education (ISTE) and the Computer Science Teachers Association (CSTA) have developed a helpful operational definition of "computational thinking" and it is closely linked to "higher thinking skills". The definition provides a framework and vocabulary for computational thinking that is intended to support all KS1–4 teachers:

Computational thinking (CT) is a problem-solving process that includes (but is not limited to) the following characteristics:

- Formulating problems in a way that enables us to use a computer and other tools to help solve them
- Logically organising and analysing data
- Representing data through abstractions such as models and simulations
- Automating solutions through algorithmic thinking (a series of ordered steps)

- Identifying, analysing, and implementing possible solutions with the goal of achieving the most efficient and effective combination of steps and resources
- Generalising and transferring this problem-solving process to a wide variety of problems.

These skills are supported and enhanced by a number of dispositions or attitudes that are essential dimensions of CT. These dispositions or attitudes include:

- Confidence in dealing with complexity
- Persistence in working with difficult problems
- Tolerance for ambiguity
- The ability to deal with open-ended problems
- The ability to communicate and work with others to achieve a common goal or solution.

Case studies of successful approaches, taking risks

So in all of this changing landscape of curriculum, pedagogy, and CPD, how are schools coping? I have included some amazing examples, approaches, and conversations throughout the chapter and in this section that I hope will be helpful! In all of these examples, pedagogy always drives the technology, never the other way around.

Flipped classrooms

The rising use in schools of online video, combined with increased pupil access to technology, has helped drive "flipped learning" methods, which aim to improve student outcomes by offering more engaging, individualised, student-driven learning opportunities. Flipped learning/classrooms are a form of blended learning in which students learn new content online typically by watching video lessons, usually at home, and what used to be homework (assigned problems) is now done in class with teachers offering more personalised guidance and interaction with students, instead of didactic teaching.

Because teachers tend to post their lessons online as homework, this frees up class time for real projects that cultivate critical twenty-first century skills, such as:

- Collaboration
- Critical thinking
- Problem solving
- Active learning
- Inquiry-based learning.

Case study

There is a useful case study on the Edfutures web site of "The Flipped Classroom – Gonville Academy" (R. Allen, February 2013) that is worth reading; it describes how flipped classrooms (arguably a flipped school) evolved in this primary school. The study illustrates broad and deep impact on outcomes that would be valued in other schools, including very high levels of engagement in staff as in pupils, real impact on the quality and quantity of work produced – extraordinary impact for some individuals – big positive impact on parental commu-nication and parental engagement, changing pedagogy, and evidence of a steady upward trend in results. There are "Key Lessons Learnt" that offer insight into the "story" and advice for schools following the flipped path, including Digital Leaders and pupils as teachers. (http://edfutures.net/The_Flipped_Classroom_-_Gonville_Academy). A range of further relevant studies can be accessed at http://edfutures.net/Technology_Strategy_Case_Studies

Approaches and conversations: coding, programming, and computational thinking

Approach to programming

"We are going back to the old programming software we used to use such as Logo. Starting now, by giving teachers time to explore through inset training, some of the programming software – over the course of the next year. We will be making these programmes available on digital equipment such as tablets, iPads, laptops and desktop computers."

(Ophelia Vanderpuye, Oakington Manory Primary School, Naace London Regional Conference, November 2013)

Logo conversation

"Logo is an interesting 'low floor and high ceiling' programming language, designed by Seymour Papert for children, not always fully appreciated by schools.

Turtle graphics will teach the user about geometry (and they won't even know it). We used a free download of MSLogo, but there are free online versions too.

We introduced higher thinking skills by putting programming tasks in context – pupils were asked to design two different but related logos for a travel company, "SunSpots" (usefully suggestive of circles), as part of a longer project. The logos were to be suitable for machine-embroidered sweatshirt logos and dynamic laser lighting displays on walls and cloud banks (the programming requirements were close enough to real-life activities to be exciting). The "dynamic lighting" element was validated via peer assessment when the pupils demonstrated their program to the class. They loved it!"

(Secondary ICT coordinator)

Approach to primary coding

Simon Widdowson, Porchester Junior School, uses primary software intended to encourage pupils to plan, design, create, publish, and play – it allows pupils to create their own activities and games. It functions in two ways – "drag and drop" and more advanced coding. He has a useful web resource, www.2diyarchive.co.uk/ – a collection of ideas, tips, and examples of schools' use.

BASIC conversation

"Lots of schools are rediscovering BASIC. I've found it's an excellent starting point for moving onto other languages, and can be useful for simple programs. BASIC is easier to learn than other programming languages – its commands are similar to English and it has a simple set of rules for entering them."

(Secondary ICT/Computing teacher)

Algorithms conversation

"Algorithms can be quite difficult to get your head around! Some of my non-specialist teachers really struggle so I do this exercise with pupils and staff – it makes it fun, sometimes hysterical! Get them to imagine they are a robot and without conferring, they have to write instructions to make a 'perfect cup of tea' – do this by playing 'Consequences' – write down 10 steps to making the perfect cup of tea (1 line, hide by folding, pass to person on right and continue 10 steps) Read out results – there will be few drinkable!

Then I get them to look at the Cheese Sandwich algorithm (see Figure 1.6) – can they find a reasonable acceptable sandwich?"

(CPD provider)

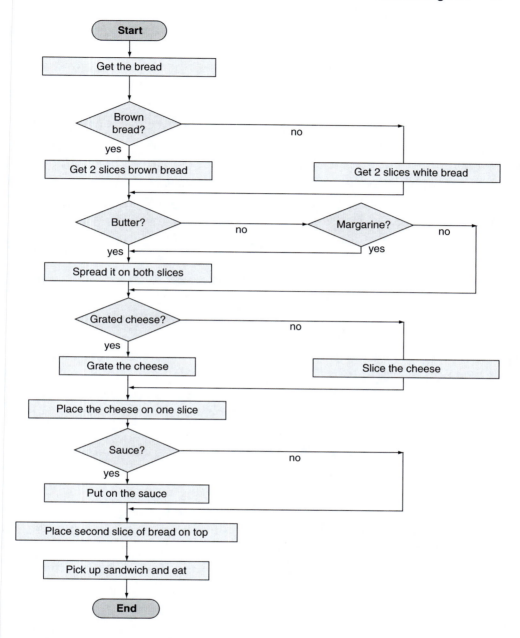

Figure 1.6 Cheese sandwich algorithm.

How computers work conversation

"I used the pilot Silicon Wafer Naace CPD resources. I found the video covering from sand to microchip really helpful for Year 9 classes. I stopped it every so often as suggested and explained briefly some of the harder concepts or to point out a particularly interesting topic. I have never seen a whole class with their mouths open – literally. I was worried about the silence – but then a buzz started and it didn't stop!

Luckily I had been given a silicon wafer and chips to show my class – they could generally make out the top 5 layers of the thousands of layers of circuits – pink, green, gold, blue were the main colours of evidence. I also showed them some silicon chips with the wiring and motherboard.

What was really impressive was how this resource really made them understand that the computer isn't a box and wires; it's a tiny thing less than half the size of my little fingernail! They realised how many daily objects use integrated circuits and how it's possible.

The most sophisticated silicon chip, a microprocessor, can contain hundreds of millions or billions of transistors interconnected by fine wires made of copper. Each transistor acts as an on/off switch, controlling the flow of electricity through the chip to send, receive and process information in a fraction of a second.

As they left the room they were still talking about it. The sheer scaling of silicon technology had astounded them.

We went on to binary switching – because they had seen how the IC or microchip uses on/off or 0 1 states, like light switches. The class worked out all the possible permutations of an 8 switch bank and we went on to other coding including ASCII.

I used this as a basis for two further projects; one on coding, programming and developing computational thinking, the other on control technologies via 'analogue and digital' and data logging.

We also used our knowledge to 'future gaze' during the Computing History topic and they got very interested in nanotechnology."

(Head of ICT Department)

Computing evolution conversations

"I thought this topic would be boring but my classes got really interested. Lots of parents could describe the days before internet and Google. Grandparents could remember when a computer took up a space the size of our Gym! One granddad came in and described taking his dog into the computer when he did night duty! Pupils were quite shocked."

(Teacher of Year 6 ICT)

"I printed off some topics and got my class to sort them in order. Nobody got them right, but they were all amazed at how changes in technology had speeded up – talked about mobile phones in their lifetime. More able pupils talked about how some items had **no history** because they were only developed recently; they were surprised that things changed faster than the history of the motor car. We video-conferenced with a couple of experts – very interesting.

What was really effective was a 'future-gazing' session. Students got really involved and designs included very clever thinking. I've one very disabled boy who comes in from time to time – he used his adapted wheelchair input device to write about a nano robot chip that could be implanted to his muscle functions. Impressive stuff!"

(Teacher of Year 9 Computing)

"We found masses of information about computer history. Some pupils experimented with coding on our very old machine. Some played 'Barrels' (*c.*1985) – loved it, wrote their own game! We printed out info, code and pics, then stuck them on talking postcards with a recorded voice-over and made a wall display. Younger kids loved it!"

(Teacher of KS3 ICT/Computing)

"Set research on computer history for homework and everyone did a presentation. My pupils sort of missed the point and it seemed to just be a list of facts. They didn't 'get' the impact of the new technologies and Moore's Law – I'll be much more adventurous! I want to try online mindmapping and maybe Flashmeeting with a school we know in New York."

(Teacher of Year 9 ICT/Computing)

"I decided to make a timeline wall. Each pupil researched a topic (lots of info on www.hoc.lgfl.net) and found or printed photos that they embedded in brief descriptions. We built the timeline across a wall in the classroom and pinned the topics up in the right 'time-zone'."

(Teacher, KS2)

Evaluation conversations

"I got my pupils to appoint a 'SID' – it means Standard IDiot Test and it's what flat-pack furniture makers are supposed to do with their instructions! It really means, get a layperson to read your evaluation report – if they can understand it – good, if they can't, it's up to the pupil to put it right! It's a good way to involve parents meaningfully and it gives pupils a real audience to write for. It only works with supportive adult readers – not at all with siblings."

(Teacher, Years 7–11)

"All my year groups attempt evaluation (all mixed ability). After a unit of work we generally do a longer project that brings everything together – at the end of a term or even half term. I set it in a context they can recognise.

I have examples around the room – some I've made up to look like pupil writing but covering essential points with red pen 'marking'. Pupils never copy but need to see what 'good' looks like. The examples have all the elements of systems design. Some able Year 7 can write like this because their literacy levels are high. Others struggle and I use questioning (very much with less able) and video for evidence. By Year 9 they're all pretty good at measurable success criteria and evaluation. I get some level 7s in Yr 7, lots in Yr 9 (and Ofsted agreed).☺"

(Head of Department, ICT)

Practical programming conversation

"I find my pupils get more out of programming and are more enthusiastic when it's to solve a real problem. For example, Visual Basic is a great text-based environment. A good 'fear free' starter is to get pupils to record a macro in any MS program – Word/Excel/PowerPoint. Power_Point can have a useful macro to make a multi-end story very engaging by allowing movement around the presentation and back easily. In Word and Excel, I often find kids don't name their work – so a simple macro to put name, form and date on the footer (as well as maybe fit to one page, etc.) at one click makes them feel super-expert! They record and put the macro button on the toolbar. By Viewing Macro, they get to understand other commands and can relatively easily edit their program. They get the point! (Beside that I have nothing to pay☺)

For G&T kids (even at KS2), I have LabVIEW installed on a limited number of machines – I'm currently using free downloads and all the online demos and video – it's so good I'm going to purchase a few copies at about £12 each (note, 2013 price – it's worth shopping round).

(Reading) 'NI LabVIEW is a graphical programming environment used on campuses all over the world to deliver hands-on learning to the classroom, enhance research applications, and foster the next generation of innovators. With the intuitive nature of graphical system design, educators and researchers can design, prototype, and deploy their applications.' (LabVIEW's what runs LEGO MINDSTORMS)

It's thrilling that they're using a real program, used worldwide in industry. In school it's simulation (but they could control all the heating and lighting in school!). The drag and drop is easy, although the wiring's trickier and each virtual instrument is built of other instruments that you can open up – and each has a wiring diagram. Do an example instrument first, then look at YouTube for ideas – play a guitar or control a greenhouse!"

(ICT teacher – "a bit of primary, KS3 and KS4")

Twenty-first century learning and 3rd Millennium Learning

In December 2013, the OECD released the five-yearly PISA results and the UK performed poorly. In 2015, participants will be tested on "collaborative problem solving" as well as reading and maths.

Amelia Peterson of the Innovation Unit posted some insightful views on necessary skills; she observed that "twenty-first century skills" – collaboration, communication, problem-solving, etc. – have been on the agenda for over a decade. As education became increasingly competitive, students were fed processed "learning" to prepare them for exams designed for bulk marking; while China, South Korea, and Singapore have been building collaboration, creativity, and communication into their curricula for several years, England seems to have stalled, fearing previous failed education reforms.

Some schools have students producing high-quality work in a way that is internationally recognised as developing the kinds of skills and outlook required for future jobs. In the USA, High Tech High schools use "project-based learning" – a method of getting students to work together on long-term, real-world projects that engage and motivate students to push themselves to higher standards. Project-based learning is named by the OECD as an example of pedagogy that develops collaborative problem solving. Despite PISA results, the UK has its own schools exemplifying twenty-first century skills, their pupils benefitting from 3rd Millennium Learning – short videos of these schools are available via www.naace.co.uk/thirdmillenniumlearningaward/schoolawardvideos. See Table 1.1 for examples from the twenty-first century learning environment.

3rd Millennium Learning

For the last 30 years, information technology has been an enabler and facilitator of education in schools. Technology-based learning emerged, extending the reach and transfer of knowledge. In the twenty-first century, schools are finding that the act of connecting ideas, people, and activities elevates learning and school improvement. This model is often called "Connected Learning" and is exemplified in Naace's 3rd Millennium Learning Award schools.

Schools that have attained the Naace 3rd Millennium Learning Award are inspirational through:

- New philosophies as well as excellent practice based on sound research
- Supporting development of higher thinking skills with Communities of Learning, pupils as creators/leading learning, well-developed learning environments, and evidence of technologies used well
- Using blogging particularly well in conjunction with Communities of Learning, global citizenship, and parental engagement.

As illustrated in the Judging Tool (Figure 1.7), 3rd Millennium Schools have embedded collaboration that breaks down cultural and organisational barriers across divisions and geographies, creating a valuable knowledge-building community for learners and schools.

Table 1.1 Twenty-first century skills

Twentieth century classroom	Twenty-first century learning environment
Time-based	Outcome-based
Focus: memorisation of discrete facts	Focus: what students know, can do, and are like after all the details are forgotten
Lessons focus on the lower level of Bloom's taxonomy – knowledge, comprehension, and application	Learning is designed on upper levels of Bloom's taxonomy – synthesis, analysis, and evaluation (and include lower levels as curriculum is designed down from the top)
Textbook-driven	Research-driven
Passive learning	Active learning
Learners work in isolation – classroom within four walls	Learners work collaboratively with classmates and others around the world – the Global Classroom
Teacher-centred: teacher is centre of attention and provider of information	Student-centred: teacher is facilitator/coach
Little to no student freedom	Great deal of student freedom
"Discipline problems" – educators do not trust students and vice versa. No student motivation	No "discipline problems" – students and teachers have mutually respectful relationship as co-learners; students are highly motivated
Fragmented curriculum	Integrated and interdisciplinary curriculum
Grades averaged	Grades based on what was learned

continued

Table 1.1 Continued

Twentieth century classroom	Twenty-first century learning environment
Time-based	*Outcome-based*
Low expectations	High expectations – "If it isn't good, it isn't done". We expect, and ensure, that all students succeed in learning at high levels. Some may go higher – we get out of their way to let them do that
Teacher is judge. No one else sees students' work	Self, peer, and other assessments. Public audience, authentic assessments
Curriculum/school is irrelevant and meaningless to the students	Curriculum is connected to students' interests, experiences, talents, and the real world
Print is the primary vehicle of learning and assessment	Performances, projects, and multiple forms of media are used for learning and assessment
Diversity in students is ignored	Curriculum and instruction address student diversity
Literacy is the 3Rs – reading, writing, and mathematics	Multiple literacies of the twenty-first century – aligned to living and working in a globalised new millennium
Factory model, based upon the needs of employers for the Industrial Age of the nineteenth century. Scientific management	Global model, based upon the needs of a globalised, high-tech society.
Driven by the NCLB and standardised testing mania	Driven by exploration, creativity, and twenty-first century skills

Source: Adapted from Futurelab (2011).

The dimensions of change

In schools where 3rd Millennium Learning is happening, we expect to see changes that are very close to the twenty-first century skills and are expressed in the Judging Tool. We do not necessarily expect to see all these changes happening as schools will focus on the most profitable changes to improve learning and increase achievement.

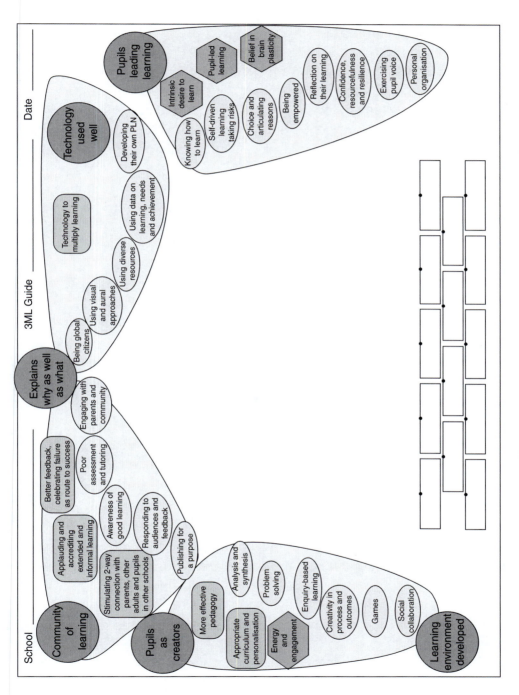

Figure 1.7 The 3rd Millennium Judging Tool (Naace 2013, http://tinyurl.com/naace3rdMllm).

1. Teacher-dependent learning changing to self-directed, lifelong, and personalised learning.
2. Twentieth-century, pre-computer, and pre-network learning skills changing to 3rd Millennium Learning skills.
3. Schools following externally imposed approaches to teaching and learning changing to schools deciding themselves what are the most appropriate approaches for their pupils and community.
4. Notions of fixed intelligence and limits in ability to learn changing to reflection on learning to develop the capacity to learn more and an understanding of brain plasticity.
5. Learning as something that happens in individual schools, classrooms, and people changing to learning that uses connections with other people to a far greater extent.
6. Learning in extrinsically imposed ways changing to learning that happens through intrinsic learning behaviours and attitudes.
7. School learning largely isolated from home learning changing to two-way parental engagement with young people's learning.
8. Accredited learning happening mainly in schools changing to extended learning.
9. The amount of creativity in teaching and learning becoming considerably greater.
10. Teachers and pupils becoming increasingly aware of, and using, the kinds of pedagogy and learning that are more effective, such as student-centred, enquiry-based learning.
   (www.naace.co.uk/thirdmillenniumlearningaward/dimensions)

We have discussed how Computing and ICT could be the most powerful enablers of transformation we possess.

In considering the "what" of Computing, and "how" we are teaching it, we must keep learning outcomes at the forefront while reviewing what we are trying to achieve:

1. Do the skills others demonstrate resonate with the range of skills we are actively trying to equip our learners with?
2. Is there a common view in our school (and understanding) of the skills needed by young people in the twenty-first century?
3. How should we articulate the skills we are seeking our learners to develop in ways which resonate with them and the local community?

4. Are these skills made explicit to teachers, learners, and parents/carers in a consistent manner?
5. Can we develop a compelling learner journey and "skills ladder" for our school?
6. When learners develop skills, do we then provide them with ample opportunities to consistently apply them across our curriculum?
7. In addition to our core curriculum, what other routes are we currently using to try and support our learners to develop these skills (e.g. enrichment activities)?

- Where have we been most successful?
- Where have we struggled or made little progress?

(Adapted from Futurelab, 2011)

References

Assessment Reform Group (1999) *Assessment for Learning: Beyond the Black Box*. University of Cambridge, Faculty of Education.

Fisher, R. (2005) *Teaching Children to Think*. Cheltenham: Nelson Thornes.

Futurelab (2011) *Resource Pack for Futurelab Hubs: Introduction to 21st Century Skills* (March). Slough, Berkshire: Futurelab Education.

Guardia, L., Maina, M., & Sangrà, A. (2013) "MOOC design principles. A pedagogical approach from the learner's perspective", *eLearning Papers*, 33 (May), 1–6.

Waters, M. (2007) "Developing and accrediting personal skills and competencies; Report and ways forward", Slough, Berkshire: Futurelab. Available online at: http://archive.futurelab.org.uk/resources/documents/project_reports/Developing_and_Accrediting_Personal_Skills_and_Competencies.pdf.

2 Philosophy and Computing

Miroslava Černochová

A rationale for teaching Computing

In schools and universities "algorithms" is a key topic in all informatics curricula.

(Futschek, 2007)

Introduction

For children, computers have become a kind of "digital playground" where they can play, think, communicate, and realise their ideas. Children who go to school do their homework using computers. Computers have become an organic part of the educational environment, and their capacity is now exploited in almost all school subjects. In some countries, a central focus in school education has been, and it still is, how to develop pupils' skills to work with the computer, how to use basic hardware and software, how to search for information from different sources, including the Internet, and how to communicate through digital networks.

Both children and their teachers have learned this basic digital literacy. However, it is high time to master much more than just how to operate a computer. It is high time to learn why and how to use computers for solving problems, and to understand what a computer can really do to serve pupils in their learning and discovering, in acquiring knowledge and abilities; how to protect and prevent her/himself against the various risks lurking in a digital world, how to behave in the right way in such a huge cyberspace. In some countries, not only in the UK, criticism of teaching focused only, or mainly, on computer-user skills development has begun (see Chapter 1) and has been met by the introduction of a new Computing curriculum.

When speaking of critical voices on the subject of how ICT has been used in school education across the world, a return to the introduction of Computing and the computer in the curriculum is often called for. It is nothing new: several years ago in some countries children were taught to program 8-bit (and later 16-bit) computers in Logo, BASIC, Karel, and so on. Nowadays, we have begun to talk again about the implementation of Computing and computer science in school education. The idea is not, however, that schools will train experts in computer programming, or produce professional computer programmers. The participants of international initiatives supported by UNESCO and IFIP agreed on the need to concentrate ICT education in schools on the development of computational thinking. "Advancing computational thinking in 21st century learning" was one of the key topics negotiated in the latest EDUsummIT[1] in Washington DC in 2013. Integration of Computing, or computer science, in the school curriculum has also been occupying the minds of teachers, computer scientists, experts in computer science, computer enthusiasts, and students who participated in the ISSEP[2] or Constructionism international conferences.

These participants embrace Seymour Papert's ideas about children learning with computers: "learning-by-making" (Papert & Harel, 1991), "technology as building material, hard fun, learning to learn, taking time – the proper time for the job, You can't get it right without getting it wrong, Do unto ourselves what we do unto our students" (Stager, 2007) and discuss why it is so important to regard Computing as a compulsory school subject, and how important computational thinking is for children's mental development, when considered as a competency that is capable of being exploited in all branches of human activity.

Merely attaining ICT literacy as an aim for school education belongs to the past. It is essential to teach children many skills: to be able to formulate problems and to select appropriate computer tools and applications; to encourage them to be able to decide independently on the appropriate use of digital technology for problem-solving; to determine whether the problem is solvable using computers; how to collect and analyse data;

how to automate data-processing and data-mining. It is, therefore, necessary to focus development on the ability to ask questions, to look for and discover links and contexts, to find relations between different phenomena or events, to inquire what depends on what, and what does not relate to what, to explain results and put them into contexts in relation to other facts. Equally, importance is given to teaching pupils to be able to identify errors in their ways of working, and the processes they use, and to verify the correctness of applied methods and actions. The integration of computational thinking is an opportunity to develop further pupils' logical thinking. It would be a mistake if we were to develop these abilities of children entirely in subjects about computers or computer science and as a part of Computing competency. The Computing initiative begun in the UK has opened up a huge amount of professional discussions in the world, directed at the same ends.

Computational thinking/computation

In the middle of the twentieth century, deriving from research and development in mathematics and computer systems, a process known as "a particular kind of calculation or application of computer technology in information processing"[3] called "computation" started to be elaborated. *"Computation"* was seen as a tool for solving equations, cracking codes, analysing data, and managing business processes. By the 1980s, *computation* had advanced to become a new method in science, joining traditional theory and experimentation. During the 1990s, *computation* advanced even further as people in many fields discovered they were dealing with information processes buried in their deep structures – for example, quantum waves in physics, DNA in biology, brain patterns in cognitive science, information flows in economic systems. *Computation* has entered everyday life, with new ways to solve problems, new forms of art, music, motion pictures, and commerce, new approaches to learning, and even new slang expressions (Denning & Martell, 2007).

Computational thinking can be developed in activities carried out both on computers and without them (later called "unplugged" in Chapter 6), through investigating how processes are managed, identifying problems in real, everyday systems, analysing and studying sets of data and questioning (Charlton & Luckin, 2012). According to J.M. Wing (2006), it is a similar way of thinking to that which professional computer scientists perform, and it is much more than having the ability to program computers.

A power to be able to apply computational thinking requires the capability to conceive abstraction, analysis, and generalisation at different levels. P. Pat (2007) declares that we cannot consider thinking which deals only with technical details about how to apply software as *computational* thinking. It would be a misinterpretation to reduce computational thinking entirely to programming activities. In line with other authors, P. Pat (ibid.) points out that a computer is not always indispensable for pupils' computational thinking development. There is a link between some concepts and knowledge from mathematics and computer science. Algorithms, data, databases, abstraction, enquiry (searching, conditions, rules and principles of Boolean algebra), data-scanning and driving technical equipment, robotics, and iteration (loops, recursion) closely relate to computational thinking. Computational thinking is not synonymous with the process of programming a computer. It is a human and natural way of thinking, and not thinking about, or with, a computer. The ability of computational thinking can be employed in all branches of human activity, including election campaigns, or creativity in arts or music.[4] There are several examples which illustrate how "computational thinking has become a critical part of elections today" (Mishra & Yadav, 2013) in the USA and in visual design.

Computational thinking is considered to be a cognitive skill which is of use to everybody (NRC, 2010) and in practically all activities. According to D. Hemmendinger (2010), the aim of teaching computational thinking is "to teach how to think like an economist, a physicist, an artist, and to understand how to use computation to solve their problems, to create, and to discover new questions that can fruitfully be explored".

It is recognised that teaching how to program a computer also contributes to the development of pupils' computational thinking. Contemporary pedagogy does not provide an answer to the question of how to approach the teaching of computational thinking to pupils. Therefore, we should draw on a philosophical basis from some other learning theories for approaches to teaching fundamental elements of computational thinking, including programming in the education of twenty-first century children. Fortunately, we can gain partly from ideas of Seymour Papert[5] and his followers – who elaborate his ideas and work in a form of the *Logo culture* – and partly from experiences and research carried out in the last 15 years.

Ideas of Logo culture[6]

Seymour Papert's ideas are still a current topic for an approach to the teaching of computational thinking development

When in the late 1960s, Wallace Feurzeig, Seymour Papert, and Alan Kay, in collaboration with MIT, were developing a programming language, Logo, in a commercial company, BBN,[7] computers were not such user-friendly machines. Users could communicate with computers using a command line. None of the authors of Logo could anticipate how many versions of Logo would be developed later, and what contemporary computers would look like. The team of Logo authors believed that not only experts and scientists but also children could work with a computer. Thanks to Logo, children could solve various types of tasks and discover, for example, a world of numbers and digits. All they needed was to write a few computer commands on the command line and a solution could be printed on a printer to make a floor turtle move. Seymour Papert wished that children working on a computer would think, and learn to learn, because "a computer can contribute to mental processes" (Papert, 1980). This is the idea we should still today strive to achieve.

The programming language Logo[8] was developed as "a potential vehicle for the transformation of education" (Agalianos *et al.*, 2006). Logo and its different versions gained in popularity in education in many countries. "In the early 1980s, Logo was introduced into mainstream education in the USA, the UK" (Agalianos *et al.*, 2006), Bulgaria, Slovakia, Hungary, Russia, and Poland.

Seymour Papert understood the process of learning by children with a computer as communication (speech) between children and the computer. According to him, the best way to achieve this is to give children an opportunity to design their ideas, and write to a computer what it should do, to put together computer programs, to "talk" to a computer. "Logo enabled children also to work with text – words, sentences and symbols. And that was a reason to name this language Logo from the Greek word, λόγος, (in a sense word, but also to formulate ideas)" (Tomcsányi, 2011, p. 20).

The computers that today's children have at their disposal at home differ radically from those used in the 1960s, not only from the point of view of their design, size, and technical specifications, but also in functions and ways of communicating with them. For all that (or for that reason), Papert's idea that a computer is an amazing machine, with which a child can learn to communicate or speak, is still a current topic for debate and a challenge for educators. Programming language is a language for learning. Programming language is a way by which children can formulate their ideas, and describe how they learn how to instruct their "toy", i.e. their computer. "Programming a computer means nothing more or less than communicating to it in a language that it and the human user can both 'understand' " (Papert, 1980, pp. 5–6). Working with computers today has been simplified, and teachers can give their attention to pupils' activities, tasks, games, or problems through which pupils will work creatively, think, and collaborate.

Most of us can see for ourselves that, on many occasions, if we give a tablet to a small child who cannot yet speak and read s/he discovers very soon how to work out how to use it. It seems to be a natural ability for a small child to handle such a device. After all, Seymour Papert was convinced that "learning to communicate with computers can be a natural process" (Papert, 1980, p. 6).

The pedagogy of Iohannes Amos Comenius

We can find the fundamental principles for pedagogy of children's computational thinking development in the ideas of outstanding thinkers of the past. One example is Iohannes Amos Comenius (1592–1670, born in Moravia), a Czech educational reformer and religious leader, who is remembered mainly for his innovations in methods of teaching. He held the view that a child's learning should be developed through education in harmony with nature. We should stimulate spontaneity and originality in children's learning, to guide them to inquire for themselves using their own understanding and interest. He was convinced that a child should understand what s/he wanted to accomplish in learning and where that learning was directed. Comenius believed that we should cultivate in children an inner desire for knowledge, and to be motivated to see learning as a journey towards wisdom. Further, that a child should gain pleasure and enjoyment from discovery, thus inspiring further learning. A child's mind identifies with the object of learning. We should encourage children to develop determination in their pursuit of learning and overcome any obstacles to their learning. Comenius supported the idea of encouraging children in their curiosity, in their spontaneity to ask questions. "Asking a question is half way to knowledge" (Kuras, 2007). Those who are not able to ask questions can learn nothing.

According to Comenius, rewards and praise can stimulate a child to be more doggedly persistent in pursuit of discovery and learning. Thus, rewards and praise play a very important role in learning. The opportunity to share the results of learning with others can stimulate a child to carry on learning. Mnemonic devices (pictures, stories, objects, etc.) can be very important for learning – these devices can help children to understand, or remember better. One very well-known principle in Comenius' pedagogy is to encourage a logical gradation of teaching: from the known to the unknown, from simple to more complex, from concrete to abstract. We should separate things and concepts into logical patterns, systems, and categories on the basis of similarities and analogy (Kuras, 2007).

Comenius (1592–1670) formulated his general pedagogical principles in a time when children wrote on slate tables and there was neither computer technology nor the Internet. Nevertheless, his principles correspond well with the ideas of Seymour Papert (born 1928).

Papert also emphasises that learning is an active process. In the process of learning, a child not only learns, but also learns how to learn. We should have in mind the key processes of knowledge acquisition as occurring in the brain, but activities should employ both the hands and the mind of a child. Language impacts on children's learning, and so we should encourage children to comment and declare what they are doing on the computer, and why they are doing it. Learning is also a social process: a child learns through social contact and interactions with parents, teachers, friends, fellow pupils, and through communities of people with similar interests.

Logo culture

Recently, we have seen how many children and adults have joined an international community grouped around the computer programming language: Scratch.[9] "With Scratch, young people can create their own interactive stories, games, animations, and simulations – and share their creations with one another online" (Resnick & Brennan, 2010). Programming in Scratch is similar to programming in Logo. It is user-friendly, and very pleasing that programs in Scratch are put together from coloured "pieces" like a puzzle (also called block coding), and thus small children who cannot read and write very well can put together a program, and run it by clicking a mouse. When children program, they are trying to teach Sprites to perform an action, dance, sing, jump, move, fly, and smile, etc. Children teach their Sprites to move in a similar way to how they explain and speak to their friends about what and how to do something. They must not only think in details about actions for Sprites, but also imagine and visualise a process and actions for each Sprite and which "pieces" (commands, loops, parameters, values, etc.) could be used. "Teaching the object to act or to 'think' can lead a child to reflect on its own actions and thinking" (Papert, 1980, p. 28).

All those who apply Papert's ideas with children in their professional practice, as teachers or in teacher education, can meet the former students, colleagues, and friends of Seymour Papert at conferences and workshops throughout the world. Papert's belief that a child's thinking and speech can be developed through programming a computer links a huge number of people across the world who apply this idea in the education of young people. This international community[10] develops a logo culture based on the idea of "*constructionism* as a 'framework for action'" (Noss, 2010). This community shares examples of good practice of constructivism and constructionism. Its members believe that learning and teaching theories for contemporary school education in the twenty-first century are missing, and that it is necessary to identify constructionist literacy and to form a base for the theory of learning design. The main question for contemporary school education is *what* to teach, because we cannot teach children in schools everything. We should teach children to be able, step-by-step and gradually, to learn for themselves what they will need for their lives. Thus, they need to learn how to learn.

According to E. Ackermann (2010), new theoretical approaches to learning should be patterned on principles of *sharing* (as a new way for co-operation and collaboration), *shifting identities* (fluid selves), *border-crossing* (expanding territorial borders), *literacies beyond print* (from write to notate to annotate), *a culture of gaming or simulating*, *a culture of makers, hackers and hobbyists*, and *a culture of "bricoleurs"*. In this way, a young generation lives and works out of school. This young generation is very self-critical, thinks in communities, and learns most *informally*, and by accident. It is cheering that some of the current young generation do not blindly and indifferently consume digital content, and all that they find on the internet, but that they are trying to be active and to do things completely different from their parents.

The Logo culture community is confident that educational programming has great importance for children's learning because it is a process based on learning by doing, in which a child must think to be able to achieve, to create a meaningful output or artefact (program, application, performance of an assigned task given achieved by a robot, etc.), and in which mistakes (and not errors) play an important role. Constructionism is employed not only in the subject of art and creative activities, but also in thinking as such.

The Logo culture community has been identified with Mitchel Resnick's key requirements on programming the environment for the development of programming skills (Table 2.1): the programming environment must be easy to get started with (*low floor*), be suitable, understandable, and appropriate for all children with different learning styles and knowledge (*wide walls*), and provide sufficient opportunities for implementing great ideas (*high ceiling*).

Such an environment for learning to program a computer should enable *hanging out* in carrying out the children's ideas and encouraging children to *think creatively*, *reason systematically*, and *work collaboratively*. Scratch meets all these requirements. These ideas are very well illustrated by a spiral schema (Rusk *et al.*, 2008; see Figure 2.1).

Table 2.1 Requirements for an educational programming environment dedicated to children

LOW FLOOR	Easy to get started with
WIDE WALLS	Technologies for all children with different learning styles and ways of knowing
HIGH CEILING	Opportunities for increasingly complex explorations over time

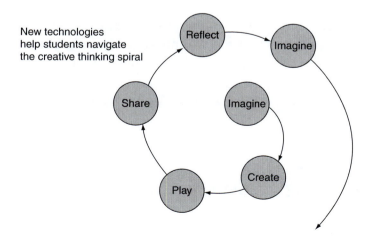

Figure 2.1 Schema of a child's creative thinking and playing (from Rusk *et al.*, 2008).

It corresponds to how small children play, create, and learn. A child usually has an idea which s/he tries to make come true and materialise. Later s/he plays with the produced artefact and shares it with other children who can change it. The result can be compared with a new idea, and with dreams. These dreams turn into a stimulus to develop in the mind a new imagined entity, which can then be created.

Programming should stimulate and evoke pleasure in, and be enjoyable for, children, equivalent to the feelings they have when they play. Playing and games belong to school education. Children can feel happy playing games. "Games are tools for rewiring your brain. When you're playing a game, what you're essentially doing is building new neurological connections, and strengthening them, with a process called myelination" (Sheely, 2014). When using Scratch (or other similar types of programming environment), children can design their own games, including their visual imagination. (See also Chapter 7: Gaming and Computing.)

Educational programming and pedagogy

The work of the Logo culture community is not aimed at putting Logo into school education, nor to educate professional programmers or ICT experts in schools. Members strive for the application of the principles of Papert's ideas and of constructionism, and to recognise the importance of computer programming for the development of children's thinking. The fact that in Slovakia, Poland, and Hungary several competitions[11] for school children in programming in Logo (mainly in Comenius Logo and Imagine-Logo) are still organised annually demonstrates that Logo continues to be very popular as a programming environment for young people. As educators, we should choose such digital environments, and arrange appropriate conditions to enable these ideas in children's learning to be realised. It does not necessarily have to be only Logo or Scratch, but we can also use other programming for children. There are several other programming tools for children which can be used in schools.

Languages of text programming on a command line (Logo and Logo descendants)

In some programming environments, it is necessary to insert – via the keyboard – both commands and programs on a command line as a combination of words, numbers, and symbols. Error reports are usually formulated as a message (or set of information) which, very often, users and programming beginners cannot understand. In such cases, beginners do not know where they made a mistake and which type of mistake they made.

Logo, Comenius Logo, and ImagineLogo (which is a new generation of developmental environment and of Logo, which belongs to a group of object-oriented programming languages) are examples of this group of programming languages. The first simple steps for understanding programming in Logo with small children can be done in EasyLogo,[12,13] which was designed for people with basic computer skills to make programming and problem solving[14] as easy as possible.

Programming in Logo has a long tradition in Slovakia. From 1991 to 1993, Comenius Logo was developed by a team of experts managed by Ivan Kalaš from Comenius University in Bratislava. Its 14 language versions spread very quickly into several countries in Europe. Later, in 1997, the same team of experts from Slovakia started to develop ImagineLogo as a successor to Comenius Logo. This also became a very popular and well-known programming language, not only in Europe but also in Latin America and Australia. This environment has been primarily dedicated to children aged from ten to 16 for the teaching of programming. The developers therefore thought about how to support children in their programming activities. For visual, animated elements, and for drawing graphic objects, children can use LogoMotion. Thanks to these simple tools, the children can very easily instruct turtles without knowing concepts like geometrical angles, and without knowledge of reading or writing at a standard level. Children can do, intuitively, a lot of things in Imagine or LogoMotion. The authors published a series of textbooks, with examples and projects on CD-ROMs for primary and secondary schools, which can help teachers and pupils to start to develop their own projects in ImagineLogo. It is understandable that ImagineLogo is very popular in Slovakia, where it was developed. In Slovakia, there are organised competitions for children in programming in ImagineLogo.[15] Teachers can find a lot of useful information about ImagineLogo on the web pages of ImagineLogo[16] or on Logotron.[17] ImagineLogo is aimed at the teaching of programming, but it can be used for professional application development too.

Programming in blocks/drag-and-drop programming language

Programming in blocks preserves a program's text. Users can drag blocks together to build a program application. Pieces of blocks fit in together as pieces of a puzzle. No typing is required.

For the first steps in programming based on drag-and-drop and blocks, we can use Blockly,[18] which is a web-based, graphical programming editor.

Snap![19] (formerly BYOB[20] – Build Your Own Blocks) was developed as a visual, drag-and-drop programming language with the support of the National Science Foundation (NSF) in USA. Users very simply do programming using drag-and-drops with the aim to put together blocks of commands and parameters. Snap!:

> *is an extended version of Scratch that allows you to Build Your Own Blocks. It also features first-class lists, first-class procedures, and continuations. These added capabilities make it suitable for a serious introduction to computer science for high school or college students.*
>
> *(http://snap.berkeley.edu/)*

Scratch[21] also belongs to this group. Currently, Scratch is, worldwide, one of the most popular environments with block structure programming for children. To some people it can resemble the Turtle Art. But there are differences between both. Scratch is an open-source project and represents object-based programming. It can quickly be used to create simple geometric shapes, or simple animations. "Scratchers" are users of Scratch. Its fascinating feature is that there is a huge international community of Scratchers connected by means of its web site. Scratch enables Scratchers:

- *to share at multiple levels of granularity, exchanging scripts, procedures, sprites, imagines, and sounds as well as projects*
- *to store "persistent data" in the cloud to create on-line surveys, high-score lists, and interaction between projects*
- *to create projects that react to movements and colours in the physical world by using the webcam as a sensor.*

(Resnick, 2013, p. 7)

Turtle Art[22] is another example from this set of programming environments. Turtle Art is a derivative programming environment of Logo, developed into a visual block version of it. It is multi-platform, and free to download (Wees, 2012).

For a better understanding of processes and phenomena around us, we can use tools for making and using models. StarLogo[23] is an example of a programmable modelling environment useful for studying "real-life phenomena, such as bird flocks, traffic jams, ant colonies, and market economies".[24]

Children will also be very attracted to programming on the iPad. It is possible to do this using, for example, Hopscotch,[25] "which allows children to do block programming in a very similar fashion to Scratch, Turtle Art, and other programming environments", or Move the Turtle:[26]

> which is an iPhone/iPad application. It has a feature set very similar to Turtle Art but with reduced programming functionality. It includes a series of tutorials through puzzles, which means that students without the support of a teacher can play around with the puzzles, and learn how the application works. Obviously, there is a certain amount of playing around necessary with any programming environment in order to learn it, but the tutorials which Move the Turtle provides are useful when students get completely stuck.
>
> (http://movetheturtle.com)

- ● **Card environment for programming**
  Card environment for programming is similar to programming in blocks. A program is put together from rectangular cards being placed next to each other and text is added only on small parts of them. Programming in cards preserves the text of the programs. Squeak[27] and Etoys[28] or Microworlds Jr. represent card environments for programming. Squeak, for example, is an open-source, full-featured implementation of the Smalltalk programming language and environment. Its virtual machine is written entirely in Smalltalk, making it easy to debug, analyse, and change. Squeak was used to create the Scratch programming system and the Etoys system (Maxwell, 2006).

- ● **Iconic programming languages**
  Programming in blocks or cards environments preserves the text of programs. The only thing is that program text is built in each of these environments in a different way.

Another approach to simplifying program composition is to eliminate text itself, using a set of icons. Nevertheless, a program still remains as a sequence of commands where some of them have parameters. The only thing is that their notation is neither text nor a construction from blocks with texts, but particular commands of program are replaced by icons (Tomcsányi, 2011, p. 37). A typical example of the iconic programming language is LEGO MINDSTORMS Education NXT.

Pedagogical approaches to teaching programming

For more than 40 years, different programming languages that could be used by children have been developed. Nevertheless, what is still missing are general theoretical works, based on research, on how a child thinks about programming and how s/he can develop programming skills, ideas, and computational thinking. There do exist some partial works, which could contribute to develop the pedagogy of programming, and push forward a theoretical basis of pedagogy of computational thinking. One of them is from Lovászová (2013), who tried to identify four fundamental concepts of teaching in programming for pupils aged 11 to 15. The pillar of her theory consists of programming paradigms, typology of problems, methods and forms of performance (work), ways of computational performance, and its visualisation put into a context of programming paradigms, and methods of how to teach children aged 11 to 15. Each of these concepts adds to the development of a theory of the forming and the development of algorithmic abilities, and computational thinking (Table 2.2).

Approaches to Computing in the curriculum

There have been recent initiatives striving to implant the basics of computer science or Computing into school education. Although these initiatives have different elements and differ in success, they represent a common interest in starting to develop the computational thinking of pupils in primary education, in some countries from pre-school education.

The introduction to computer science, including programming, can be through curricular change in school education for children aged from six to 15 either as a separate subject, as with other school subjects, or as a meta-subject for laying the foundations for other subjects. The first approach is realised in some EU countries and it is sometimes joint with teaching mathematics (for example, in Slovakia); the second, with a model of computer science in the role as a meta-subject, has been carried out in Russia.

Teaching of computer science as a part of mathematics education

Slovakia has always put an emphasis on teaching computation or computer science in school education. ICT literacy and user skills have been developed partly in computer science education, partly in the teaching of other school subjects in creative activities, or solving problems. From 2008, education in Slovak schools follows a set of curricular documents of governmental educational programmes (Štátny vzdelávací program, acronym ŠVP) for pre-school education,[29] primary education,[30] lower secondary education,[31] and secondary education.[32] Based on this governmental document, each school develops its own school educational programme.

It is a great success. "It succeeded in bringing together educational reform and a process of computerisation and established computing and computational education as new subjects into curriculum ŠVP" (Blaho, 2011) and to begin Computing in pre-school education, in kindergarten. For primary education (aged 6–15) and secondary education (aged 15–19), it is common that computational education comes into being as a subject, Informatics, which when combined with mathematics creates the subject *Mathematics and work with information*. The educational content for Informatics is divided into five thematic units, although each unit plays a different key role on different levels of education: (1) Information around us; (2) Procedures, methods, and problem-solving; algorithm thinking; (3) Communication through ICT; (4) Principles of ICT operation; (5) the information society. Students who would like to graduate from secondary school can do a final-year examination on Informatics in which they must provide evidence of theoretical knowledge and practical skills in Computing and also in the use of ICT.[33]

In Slovakia, basic concepts of computational education are integrated into pre-school education in kindergartens. All kindergarten teachers have been trained in pedagogy for propaedeutic (preparatory) computational education for pre-school pupils. Computational education in the kindergarten acknowledges the stages of mental development of children, and is focused mainly on robotics and the programming of digital toys (Kalaš,

Table 2.2 Concepts of a pedagogical approach to teaching programming (by Lovászová, 2013, and Gujberová & Tomcsányi, 2013)

Concept	Description	
Concept based on a metaphor of turtle in programming language Logo as a symbol of educational paradigm (Lovászová, 2013)	In schools, we can use for teaching programming different versions of Logo, Comenius Logo or ImagineLogo, or Scratch. Teaching is very often concentrated on turtle geometry. Fine Arts can inspire teachers to formulate questions or assignments for children to do. According to this concept, we can utilise also programmable robotic toys (Bee-Bot etc.) to design "lively pictures"[a], stories, objects and games, or the Drawing Robot.	Languages of text programming on a command line. Programming in blocks/drag-and-drop programming language
Concept based on spreadsheet (Lovászová, 2013)	Two-dimensional spreadsheets can serve as an example, to some degree, of programming. Each table/sheet containing a formula is in fact a program. Sometimes we speak about "live/animated sheets". Work with spreadsheets encourages abstract thinking and the development of algorithmic thinking. Using spreadsheets, a pupil can visualise a process of computation and identify an error in algorithms.	Mainly languages of text programming in a command line
Concept based on programming specialised robots (Gujberová & Tomcsányi, 2013)	"The robot can move and sense walls. It can put and collect marks (beepers), in newer implementations it can also put and collect bricks. The programs are written in text form, it includes procedures. It has no variables" (Gujberová & Tomcsányi, 2013). For example, Karel, Karel 3D for Win 32, Baltie, Jumper, Phillip the Ant.	Programs are written in text form

Concept based on advanced environments (Gujberová & Tomcsányi, 2013)	For example, Microsoft Kodu Game Lab (Kodu), which has been designed for creating and playing one's own games. The conditions and commands are expressed by icons selected from menus (repositories). Alice 3D "allows creating animations, interactive stories, videos and games" (Gujberová & Tomcsányi, 2013)	The conditions and commands are expressed by icons selected from menus
Concept based on robotic toys and programmable robotic kits (Lovászová, 2013)	For these purposes, we can use, for example, LEGO MINDSTORMS NXT.	Mainly Iconic programming languages
Concept based on using mobile technology (Lovászová, 2013)	This approach is based on activities with mobile digital technology which can be organised out of school as field-trip activity. Children can be involved in navigation games with mobile digital devices in which a player plays the role of a processor in real time and in which his/her movement is recorded and scanned by means of GPS. Other types of activities are based on drawing with GPS and field games in which players work with geographical data about a player's position. We can use a Urwigo system or a Wherigo platform.	Mainly programming in blocks/drag-and-drop programming language

Note
a The term "lively pictures" is taken from Gujberová & Tomcsányi (2013).

2010). The pre-school concepts are gradually developed in primary, later at lower secondary, and then at secondary education level. Slovakia has been successful in making good use of about 25 years' experience with informatics education, concepts of programming in Logo, Comenius Logo and Imagine. ICT is still a part of the teaching of computational education and computer science in the curriculum. Nevertheless, in the context of the revision of general and specific goals and the implementation of output and content standards for computer science, there is an attempt "to move the goals of teaching computer science in the opposite direction: from ICT to data representation, informatics' language and to solving problems" (Blaho, 2011).

At the time of writing, the pursuit of goals in Computing education is hampered by a *misunderstanding* of the real purpose of informatics, a *non-professional view* on what informatics really means, and what the difference is between informatics and ICT and by the fact that pupils have sometimes much more experience with some areas of computer science than their teachers (Blaho, 2011).

It was a team of experts and doctoral students managed by Professor Ivan Kalaš from the Comenius University in Bratislava that played a great part in the success of the strategy for informatics and computer science, including the production of textbooks, teacher guides and computer applications, and programming environments for schools and teachers in Slovakia.

Informatics as a meta-subject

The bases of a computer science or Computing education are already included in the school curriculum in Russia[34] as a meta-subject in primary education. Learning outcomes achieved at this level are developed later, not only in mathematics and informatics, but also in language education at the lower secondary education level. The idea of a propaedeutic approach to computational thinking development of primary school children was designed by Professor Alexej Semenov in Moscow more than 20 years ago.

In the curriculum for primary education, there are two educational areas: *Mathematics and informatics* and *Technology*.

● *Mathematics and informatics* is focused on the development of ICT abilities from the computer science perspective. Pupils learn through topics such as *Work with information* (the structure of simple logical propositions using logical expressions [and, if, true statement – false statement]), *Creation, transcript and analysis of algorithms, reading, data-filling and interpretation from spreadsheets*.

- The unit *Practical exercise with computers*, as a part of *Technology*, is dedicated to practice of how to work with digital information, rules for keeping healthy and safe when using computers, the basis of work with text-processing with office applications. In primary education, the main focus is working with ICT, safety with ICT, technology for getting and saving (text, numerical, sound, and graphic) data on computers, and searching and processing information. Pupils are expected to be able to create, present and share information, and plan and manage activities. The unit *Designing and modelling* is focused on simple procedures on how to use computers for designing and modelling using interactive constructive environments.

At the lower secondary education level, both educational areas *Mathematics and informatics* and *Technology* contribute to computational knowledge and skills.

- *Mathematics and informatics* is focused on key concepts, principles, and procedures from computer science and informatics as a base for pupils' computational and algorithmic culture development. The subject *Informatics* contributes especially to the formation of ideas about the computer as a universal, all-purpose device for information processing and to basic skills of how to use a computer. Much attention is given to the development of algorithmic thinking and the ability to produce transcripts of algorithms for solving real situations, and to the active use of one programming language. Pupils learn to use algorithmic structures (linear, conditioned, and cyclical). Computational education is aimed also at the development of skills to formalise and structure information, and to select an appropriate means of data representation in a specific context in an assigned task, using appropriate software applications for data processing.
- *Technology* implemented in Years 6–8 is focused on skills in the use of ICT, the ability to evaluate and select appropriate software and ICT tools in various activities and to develop ideas about ICT usage in different careers.

Conclusion

With regard to the development of computational thinking and algorithmic skills through teaching programming language in school education, there are listed below – and cogently summarised by Ivan Kalaš (Kalaš *et al.*, 2011) – a number of principles, which reflect Papert's philosophy, and which the community of Logo culture has adopted:

1. *Learning is an active process* in which a child explores his or her senses and, thanks to them, s/he constructs in her/his mind meanings and concepts.
2. *When a child learns, s/he, at the same time, learns to learn* – metacognitive skills are inseparable from the learning process.
3. Key moments for the knowledge process are *forming in a mind* – activities must occupy both the hands (body) and the mind.
4. *Language has an influence on learning* – both these phenomena are inseparable.
5. *Learning is a social activity* – a child learns in a social context in collaboration and interaction with others (parents, grandparents, siblings, close relatives, teachers, schoolmates, friends, etc.).
6. *Learning depends on context* – a child does not learn abstract, isolated, and separated knowledge but things which relate to her/his life.
7. A child cannot learn without building on her/his previous knowledge. In a process of *construction of a new "live" knowledge*, it is very important that it fits into and engages with a mental construct.
8. *Learning requires time* – very often we must return to some ideas and think about them, verify them, and play with them for them to become part of our real "live" understanding and knowledge. We should pay attention to the planning of long-term activities and engagement.
9. *Motivation is a key part of learning*. It develops from the learner's interests – if we don't know why we are learning, we shall not understand where and how to apply our knowledge and learning and then new knowledge loses sense for us.
10. *Hard fun and playful learning* – problems, tasks, or exercises should be sufficiently playful, simple, and understandable to be attractive for a child, but also hard enough to keep his/her attention and interest.
11. *Opportunity to make mistakes and learn from them* – do not forget to give our children space for their own solution in which they will very

often make mistakes. Through dialogue with children, we can identify why they made a mistake and how to help them.

12. *Teamwork, collaboration, and roles in a team* – children can learn how to organise work in teams and how to divide tasks: it is not possible to solve some problems without the help of others.

13. *Teachers are also learners and learn* – it is impossible for teachers to be ready for solving all problems which can arise, so they very often solve unforeseen problems and, together with their pupils, learn new things.

In schools, we should strive to accomplish these principles in order to establish playfully amazing learning environments for our pupils, where they can feel happy; where they will be safe; where they will learn to learn; where they will enjoy learning, collaborating, and being creative.

Notes

1. www.edusummit.nl/.
2. Informatics in Schools: Situation, Evolution and Perspectives.
3. http://en.wikipedia.org/wiki/Computation.
4. For example, in the Workshop in Algorithmic Computer Music (WACM), participants can learn how to apply a programming language, LISP, for music composition (http://arts.ucsc.edu/programs/wacm/).
5. www.papert.org/works.html.
6. www.microworlds.com/support/logo-philosophy-papert.html.
7. Bolt, Beranek and Newman, Inc.
8. P. Boytchev (2011) in his Logo Tree Project keeps a record of about 230 catalogued versions of Logo.
9. http://scratch.mit.edu/.
10. This community is represented by experts from Bulgaria (Evgenia Sendova, Pavel Boytchev, Vessela Ilieva, Nikolina Nikolova, etc.), Brazil (Leonardo Cunha de Miranda, Fábio Ferrentini Sampio, etc.), Canada (Paula Bontá, Brian Silverman, etc.), Costa Rica (Eleonora Badilla-Saxe, etc.), the Czech Republic (Jiří Vaníček, Miroslava Černochová), France (Carol-Ann Braun, Ioana Cristina Ocnarescu, etc.), Germany (Michael Weigend, etc.), Greece (Dimitris Alimisis, Chronis Kynigos, etc.), Hungary (Marta Turcsányi-Szabó, Otilia Pasaréti, etc.), Israel (Sharona T. Levy, etc.), Lithuania (Tatjana Balvočiené, etc.), Mexico (Jesús Jimenéz-Molotla, Ana Isabel Sacristán, Cristianna Butto-Zarzar, Alejandro Rosas, etc.), Poland (Maciej Syslo, Agnieszka Borowiecka, Maciej Borowiecki, Katarzyna Oledzka, etc.), Russia (Alexej Semenov, Boris Berenfeld, etc.), Slovakia (Ivan Kalaš, Andrej Blaho, Lubomir Salanci, Peter Tomcsányi, Martina Kabátová, Janka Pekárková, etc.), South Korea (Han Hyuk

Cho, Hwa Kyung Kim, etc.), UK (Richard Noss, Dave Pratt, Jo Cole, David Ryan Smith, Artemis Papert, etc.), USA (Mitchel Resnick, E.K. Ackermann, Wallace Feurzeig, Brian Harvey, Uri Wilensky, Gary S. Stager, Artemis Papert, Eric Neumann, Dorothy M. French, Viera K. Proulx, etc.), etc.

11. ImagineLogo Cup, Palma Junior, LOGIA, miniLOGIA, POLLOGIA, Logo Orszá-gos Számítástechnikai Tanulmányi Verseny.
12. http://edi.fmph.uniba.sk/~salanci/EasyLogo/index.html.
13. Lubomir Salanci from Comenius University in Bratislava (Slovakia) is the author of EasyLogo.
14. Some ideas and tasks to be solved are on http://edi.fmph.uniba.sk/~salanci/ EasyLogo/Paper.pdf.
15. http://edi.fmph.uniba.sk/~tomcsanyiova/ImagineLogoCup/index.php.
16. http://imagine.input.sk/international.html.
17. www.r-e-m.co.uk/logo/?Titleno=19015.
18. http://code.google.com/p/blockly/?redir=1.
19. http://snap.berkeley.edu/run. On http://snap.berkeley.edu/snapsource/snap. html you can get first experiences with it. It would be very easy for you to work with Snap! if you have some experience with Scratch.
20. http://byob.berkeley.edu/.
21. http://scratch.mit.edu.
22. http://turtleart.org/programming/index.html.
23. http://education.mit.edu/starlogo/, www.stem-works.com/external/activity/215.
24. http://education.mit.edu/starlogo/adventures/intro.pdf.
25. http://davidwees.com/content/programming-kids.
26. http://movetheturtle.com/.
27. www.squeak.org/.
28. www.squeakland.org/.
29. Štátny vzdelávací program. ISCED 0 – predprimárne vzdelávanie. Štátny ped-agogický ústav. Bratislava, 2008.
30. Štátny vzdelávací program pre 1. stupeň základnej školy v Slovenskej repub-like. ISCED 1 – primárne vzdelávanie. Štátny pedagogický ústav. Bratislava, 2009.
31. Štátny vzdelávací program pre 2. stupeň základnej školy v Slovenskej repub-like. ISCED 2 – nižšie sekundárne vzdelávanie. Štátny pedagogický ústav. Bratislava.
32. Štátny vzdelávací program pre gymnázia v Slovenskej republike. ISCED 3A – Vyššie sekundárne vzdelávanie. Štátny pedagogický ústav. Bratislava.
33. Cieľové požiadavky na vedomosti a zručnosti maturantov z informatiky. Štátny pedagogický ústav. Bratislava, 2010.
34. Федеральный закон Российской Федерации N 273-ФЗ «Об образовании в Российской Федерации» принят от 29 декабря 2012 г.

Bibliography

Ackermann, E. (2010) "Constructivism(s): shared roots, crossed paths, multiple legacies". In J.E. Clayson & I. Kalaš (eds) *Constructionism 2010. Constructionist Approaches to Creative Learning, Thinking and Education: Lessons for the 21st Century*. Paris: AUP.

Agalianos, A., Whitty, G., & Noss, R. (2006) "The social shaping of Logo", *Social Studies of Science*, 36: 241. Available at: http://sss.sagepub.com/content/36/2/241.full.pdf+html.

Blaho, A. (2011) "Informatika v Štátnom vzdelávacom programme". In G. Andrejková (ed.) *Sborník DIDINFO 2011*. Banská Bystrica: Univerzita Mateja Bela.

Boytchev, P. (2011) "Logo Tree Project", July. Available at: http://recursostic.educacion.es/secundaria/edad/4esotecnologia/quincena12/pdf/Logo_Tree Project.pdf.

Charlton, P., & Luckin, R. (2012) "Time to re-load? Computational thinking and Computer Science in schools", "What the Research Says" Briefing 2, 27 April. Available at: www.lkl.ac.uk/cms/files/jce/articles/time_to_re-loadwhattheresear chsaysbriefing27april2012.pdf.

Computer Science Principles Performance Assessment (2013) The College Board. National Science Foundation.

Denning, P.J., & Martell, C. (2007) "Great principles of Computing", 18 June. Available at: http://denninginstitute.com/pjd/GP/gp_overview.html.

Ďurina, D., Petrovič, P., & Balogh, R. (2006) "Robotnačka – The Drawing Robot", *Acta Mechanica Slovaca*, 2-A/2006.

Федеральный закон Российской Федерации N 273-ФЗ «Об образовании в Российской Федерации» принят от 29 декабря 2012 г.

Futschek, G. (2007) "Logo-like learning of basic concepts of algorithms – having fun with algorithms", *Proceedings, EUROLOGO*, Bratislava, 2007. S. 2.

Gujberová, M., & Tomcsányi, P. (2013) "Environments for programming in primary education", *Informatics in Schools: Local Proceedings of the 6th International Conference, ISSEP 2013 – Selected Papers*, 53–60. Available at: http://opus. kobv.de/ubp/volltexte/2013/6368/pdf/cid06.pdf.

Hemmendinger, D. (2010) "A plea for modesty", *ACM Inroads*, 1(2), 4–7.

Kalaš, I. (2010) "Recognising the potential of ICT in early childhood education", Analytical survey, UNESCO Institute for Information Technologies in Education.

Kalaš, I., Kabátová, K., Mikolajová, K., & Tomcsányi, P. (2011) "Konštrukcionizmus od Piageta po školu v digitálnom veku", Keynote speech, DIDINFO 2011, Banská Bystrica.

Kuras, B. (2007) *Slepování střepů Komenského návrat*. Pardubice: Wald Press.

Lovászová, G. (2013) "Programovanie v sekundárnom vzdelávaní", Doctoral thesis. Bratislava: University Comenius in Bratislava.

Maxwell, J.W. (2006) "Tracing the Dynabook: a study of techno-cultural transformations", Ph.D. dissertation, University of British Columbia. Available at: http://tkbr.ccsp.sfu.ca/dynabook/.

Mishra, P., & Yadav, A. (2013) "Of art and algorithms: rethinking technology and creativity in the 21st century", *TechTrends*, May/June, 57 (3), 10–14.

Noss, R. (2010) "Reconstructing constructionism". In J.E. Clayson & I. Kalaš (eds) *Constructionism 2010. Constructionist Approaches to Creative Learning, Thinking and Education: Lessons for the 21st Century*. Paris: AUP.

NRC (2010). "Report of a workshop on the scope and nature of computational thinking", Washington, DC: The National Academies Press.

Papert, S. (1980) *Mindstorms. Children, Computers and Powerful Ideas*. New York: Basic Books.

Papert, S., & Harel, I. (1991) "Situating constructionism". Available at: www.papert.org/articles/SituatingConstructionism.html.

Pat, P. (2007) "Computational thinking: a problem-solving tool for every classroom", PowerPoint presentation, NECC, Atlanta 2007. Available at: www.cs.cmu.edu/~CompThink/resources/talks.html.

Resnick, M. (2013) "Stories from the Scratch community". In N. Reynolds, M. Webb, M.M. Syslo, & V. Dagiené (eds) *Learning While We Are Connected*. Volume 3: *Book of Abstracts*, 10th IFIP World Conference on Computers in Education, Toruň, Poland, 1–7 July 2013.

Resnick, M., & Brennan, K. (2010) "Getting to know Scratch". In J.E. Clayson & I. Kalaš (eds) *Constructionism 2010. Constructionist Approaches to Creative Learning, Thinking and Education: Lessons for the 21st Century*. Paris: AUP.

Rusk, N., Resnick, M., Berg, R., & Pezalla-Granlund, M. (2008) "New pathways into robotics: strategies for broadening participation", *Journal of Science Education and Technology*, 17(1), 59–69. Available at: http://web.media.mit.edu/~mres/papers/NewPathwaysRoboticsLLK.pdf.

Sheely, E. (2014) "How can knowledge be transferred from games and applied into career performance?" Available at: www.gamification.co/2014/01/07/how-gameplay-transfers-knowledge-into-skills/?goback=.gde_1146517_member_5827172060991881218#!

Stager, G. (2007) "An investigation of constructivism in the Maine Youth Centre", Ph.D. dissertation, University of Melbourne.

Tomcsányi, P. (2011) "Prostredie pre vývoj malých edukačných interaktívnych aktivít", Dizertačná práca. FMFI UK v Bratislave, 2011.

Wees, D. (2012) "Programming with 3rd graders", *The Reflective Educator*, 14 June. Available at: http://davidwees.com/content/programming-3rd-graders.

Wing, J.M. (2006) "Computational thinking", *Communications of the ACM*, March, 49 (3), 33–35. Available at: http://cs.gmu.edu/cne/pjd/GP/Wing06.pdf.

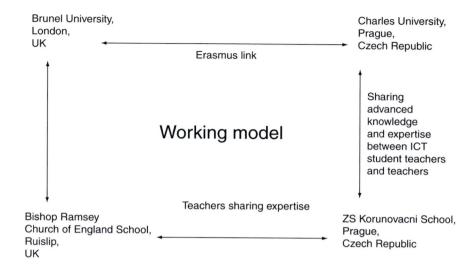

Brunel University,
London,
UK

Erasmus link

Charles University,
Prague,
Czech Republic

Working model

Sharing
advanced
knowledge
and expertise
between ICT
student teachers
and teachers

Teachers sharing expertise

Bishop Ramsey
Church of England School,
Ruislip,
UK

ZS Korunovacni School,
Prague,
Czech Republic

Figure 3.1 How Literacy from Scratch developed.

All of this work is posted, with more detailed lesson plans and examples of students' stories, on the web site: www.literacyfromscratch.org.uk.

These Scratch files can be downloaded, so that the coding can be examined and used, rather like worked solutions in mathematics. They should be used in conjunction with the relevant chapters (3, 4, and 5) in this book.

Historical note

The project was actually developed in "reverse order", starting with KS3, at Bishop Ramsey Church of England School in Ruislip, and developed further at KS2 by Brunel trainees as part of their Curriculum Enhancement course for QTS. The success of this work inspired the development of the project for much younger pupils for KS1 at Swaminarayan School in Neasden. Developments in using Art, in Prague, later inspired and fed back into the work of pupils in London. This new work is posted on the World Ecitizens web site: www.worldecitizens.net/.

Using Scratch at Key Stage 1

In this section, we will be exploring what is possible regarding the very early introduction of the Literacy from Scratch teaching and learning project for pupils aged five and six years. The work described took place at a primary school, Swaminarayan School, with the active support of the head teacher, Mr Raja, and two of his class teachers. These were Donna Roberts (a Year 1 teacher) and Francis Naera (a Year 2 teacher).

The model is based on the work carried out at KS2 and KS3, and we wanted to see how far pupils could develop their elementary computer programming skills, at ages five and six – a tall order!

The statutory guidance in set out in bold below to show which elements are met by using the Literacy from Scratch approach.

Subject content

Key Stage 1

Pupils should be taught to:

- **understand what algorithms are, how they are implemented as programs on digital devices, and that programs execute by following precise and unambiguous instructions**
- **create and debug simple programs**
- **use logical reasoning to predict the behaviour of simple programs**
- **use technology purposefully to create, organise, store, manipulate, and retrieve digital content**

and to:

- recognise common uses of information technology beyond school
- use technology safely and respectfully, keeping personal information private; identify where to go for help and support when they have concerns about content or contact on the internet or other online technologies

Year 1 Literacy from Scratch project

This teaching group had already started work on a series of lessons in the computer room, based around developing basic computer skills, such as using a mouse, logging on to the network, and controlling simple text. It was felt that this series of seven lessons should be completed before the pupils started work on Literacy from Scratch.

Step 1

Learning the basics of using a computer on the school network

Here is a sample from the introduction to ICT lesson 1 (of seven) at the Swaminarayan School:

Introduction: Discuss the parts of the computer and what they are used for. Discuss the role of the mouse. Talk about the difference between the mouse on a computer and using a laptop. When moving the mouse around, it is important to control the movement of the hand. Sudden movements will cause the mouse to jump and be momentarily lost.

Activity: Get pupils to log on to the computers and find a suitable program, e.g. Charlie Chimp (Crystal ICT program). Children work independently to dress Charlie Chimp, practising hand and eye co-ordination.

Plenary: What points must we remember when controlling the pointer? What happens when you use sudden jerky movements?

The full set of seven lesson plans is posted on the Literacy from Scratch web site.

Step 2

Planning a short narrative, in English lessons

See Figure 3.2.

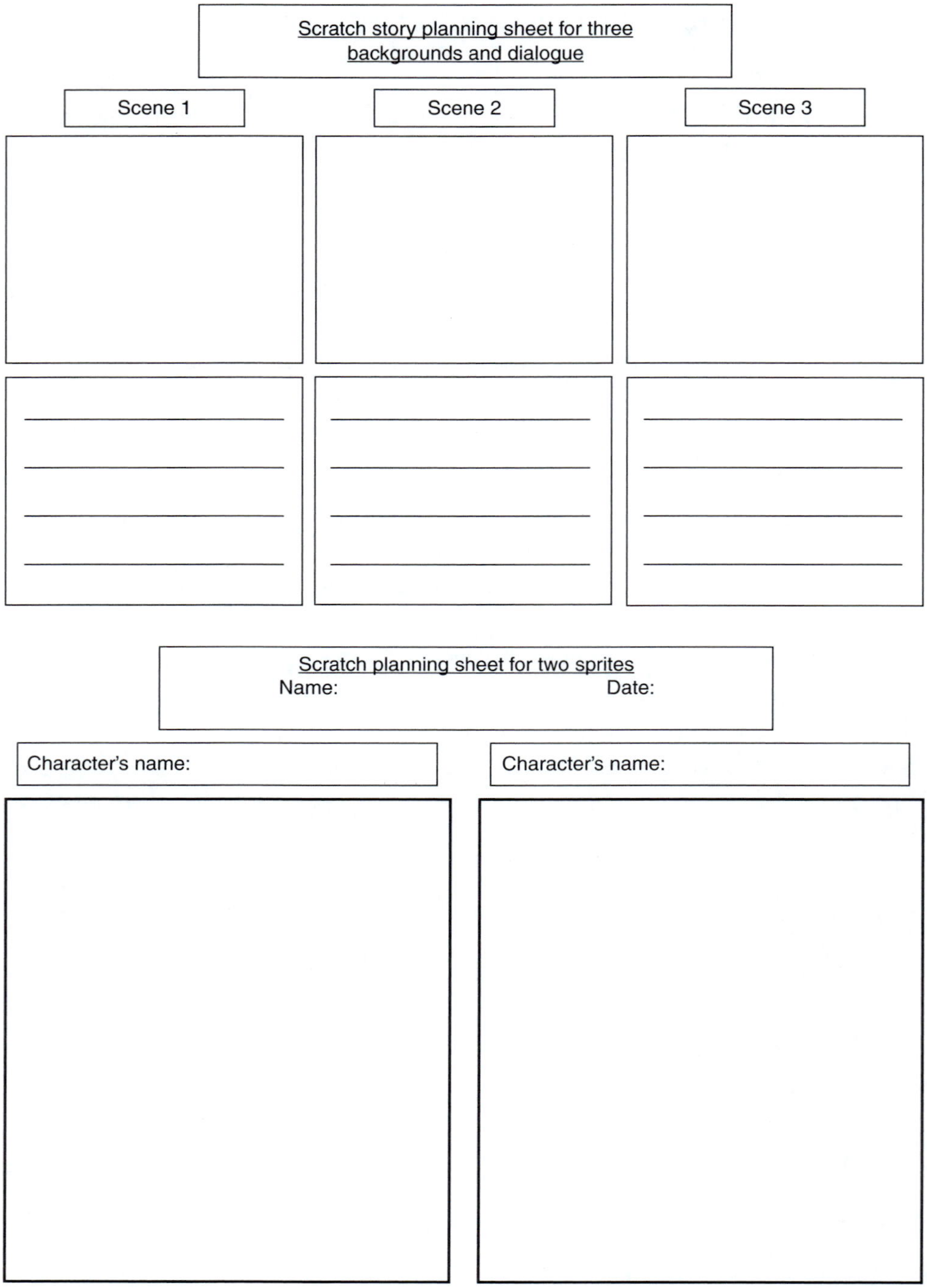

Scratch story planning sheet for three
backgrounds and dialogue

Scene 1	Scene 2	Scene 3

Scratch planning sheet for two sprites
Name: Date:

Character's name: Character's name:

Figure 3.2 Planning three scenes and related dialogue.

Year 2

As this class already had some familiarity with basic skills from their Year 1 ICT Programme of Study, we decided to launch straight into the project.

Lesson 1: Introduction to Scratch

At this stage, it was decided that the Year 2 pupils should create their own Sprites and Backgrounds, as the pupils had done in the primary school in Prague.

Francis then developed their story plans, in their subsequent English lessons.

There are several aspects of Scratch which need to be introduced, lesson by lesson.

What makes a good story, in Scratch?

Structure

Beginning: Introduce your characters and your setting.
Middle: Develop the story so that it leads up to an exciting climax.
Ending: A resolution, or happy ending, with a moral.

In Scratch, you can place a sentence of narrative across the bottom of each "page". More simply, a Title page or The End page can be added to create a more polished final story.

Setting

In Scratch, you do not actually need to describe the setting, but you can make your own "Backgrounds" against which the story will unfold. Use Draw or Paint.

Characters

Characters: In Scratch, you do not need to describe your characters, but you can show their thoughts and emotions in two ways:

● Speech bubbles

● Thought bubbles (they may not be thinking what they are actually saying...)

You can use or modify Sprites from Scratch, or from the internet, but you can also create your own. Have fun animating your characters! (These variants in movement are called "Costumes".)

Music files

You can add music files to add atmosphere to your story. You can use the files from Scratch or from the internet, but you can also create your own music, using your school's music software. You can also play an instrument and record the sound directly into Scratch.

Voice-overs

You can use a microphone to add the conversations spoken by the characters in your story. These can be in a second language, so that while the characters "speak" in English (using speech bubbles), the voice-over can be in a different language – for example, in French or Gujarati. Practical point: While reading the dialogue as a voice-over in English can be carried out at a natural speaking speed, when adding a voice-over translation, in French or Gujarati, dialogue timings need to be made longer.

Following this planning work, in English lessons, the pupils can be shown the relevant aspects of coding in Scratch. These include:

● Moving between the scenes (or Backgrounds)
● Making Sprites (or characters) move
● Making Sprites "speak" or "think"

Each element can be shown to the class, lesson by lesson, where the idea of building a wall provides a useful analogy. The coding boxes in Scratch represent the bricks of the wall, which can then be joined together.

Donna writes:

My Year 1 class
Lessons to develop the Key Stage 1 materials for the "Literacy from Scratch" project were taught by the Year 1 and 2 classroom teachers at

Swaminarayan School, West London, and took place in a fully equipped ICT suite over a timetabled lesson of one hour each week.

Students at the school are very motivated learners, but are quite varied in their existing abilities with ICT equipment, and the frequency of its use at home. Some parents are generally apprehensive about allowing their child to use a computer at home, so those students arrive at school with limited skills and experience. Some children, on the other hand, have their own iPad or laptop, and so they have far greater experience in ICT usage, and are even able to teach me a thing or two!

It was with some trepidation, therefore, that I agreed to assist Lawrence with his trials in developing a scheme of work to be used within schools, based around computer programming. I have never had any experience with programming before, and so I was apprehensive about the task ahead, and the abilities the students would be able to demonstrate, at such a young age. This, of course, was the purpose of the project!

For Year 1 students, in the first few weeks of ICT lessons, the focus had been extensively on being aware of various aspects of a computer and being able to log on and off the school system. They were then being asked to jump straight into using the Scratch program – a daunting task for any five year old, not to mention their teacher with a distinct lack of computer programming experience!

We found that the foundation of basic ICT skills, which I normally teach, still needed to be there. Each week, we would go through the steps of logging on, so that all the students would have that knowledge ingrained, and be able to increase their speed in order for there to be a noticeable progression in their learning. We introduced them to the concept of Scratch after a couple of foundation lessons in *Microsoft Word* and a Paint-like program called *Granada Colours*, already available on the school network, and a part of my introduction to computers at the school. Most of the children were, by that stage, able to log on and off the computers, open a program from a list, and select the tools they required to complete an activity (such as "draw a winter scene" or be able to change font, size, and colour when writing in *Word*). In order to set up the foundation base of knowledge to introduce the ideas of the Scratch program, students were asked to create characters in *Granada Colours* based on familiar stories, texts being studied in English, or their own imaginations. This was to inform their abilities in creating "Sprites" in Scratch.[1] Some more able students were shown how to save their work within the school's directory in their own folder.

During a week of English lessons, the Year 1 class completed a study of a text and were required to create their own versions of a story, in which a toy was lost. In the stories created in English lessons, the two main characters were the pupils themselves, and their toy. There was to be a setting for the beginning of the story; a second scene when the toy was lost (middle); and a final scene when the toy was found (ending). Each child published a mini-book of their story throughout the course of the week. Lawrence and I decided this would form a useful basis for their Scratch projects, as it suited the structure of what they were required to do. We recommend this approach: starting with a literary stimulus, prior to creative responses in writing, then move on to their Scratch stories.

After the first half-term at school, students were introduced to the Scratch program. At this stage, the children were now able to log on and off the computer efficiently, and to open the Scratch program. The first lesson concentrated on creating the Sprites in the Paint editor section of Scratch. The students were able to do this due to their experience with *Granada Colours* and the similarity of the tools and their icons used in Scratch. By the end of this lesson, the students were able to draw two Sprites from the storybooks they had previously created, and saved their Scratch project in an appropriate directory.

The subsequent lesson was used to complete the Sprites in the Paint editor, if they had not already done so, and to introduce the students to the concept of the "Stage" and creating a Background. This was an abstract concept, made more concrete to the students due to the links made through discussion about puppet shows, which they had completed in English earlier in the term, and in which I created a "background" (small b for normal use!) for each puppet show, and the children performed on the "stage" using puppets (i.e. 'Sprites'). The previous puppet show learning in English was invaluable here, as it helped form concrete links for the students with regards to what we were attempting to create in Scratch. We used Paint to create the Backgrounds, and save them. Backgrounds should be kept very simple, with perhaps just two blocks of colour – for example, blue sky and green grass, or coloured wallpaper and brown flooring. This keeps the design from intruding, when the Sprites are added. The Sprites can be more easily seen against a simple Background. It also saves time. The pupils can subsequently redevelop these Backgrounds to add further details, such as clouds, a window, or a door, once the position of the Sprites is finalised. This could be an Extension Activity for faster pupils.

The following week, we asked the students to import their Paint files from where they had saved them on the network into Scratch, in order for them to become useable Backgrounds within their projects.

Over the course of the following two weeks, students all completed their two Sprites and imported their three Backgrounds from the directory in which they saved it. More able students worked with Lawrence and me, experimenting with movement and giving commands to the Sprites. The importance of saving work became very apparent to a couple of students who did not remember, and were perplexed when they could not access their work the following week – a very valuable lesson to learn!

Students then worked towards giving their Sprites movement commands (Motion coding blocks) and adding dialogue to bring their stories to life – while always remembering to save!

In summation, I never thought that five-year-old students would be able to progress as quickly, and with as much innovation, enthusiasm, and focus as my students have. They are all so proud of their work, and we hope our experience will aid you in assisting your students along their Scratch journeys towards success in the new Computing curriculum. The best advice I can give you is to embrace the concept of programming, and allow your students to work at their own pace, while giving them enough skills and information in order for you to give support to the ones who require it, while allowing the more able children the freedom to explore their abilities through the knowledge they possess and develop. At times, quite frankly, this process has been frustrating, with multiple hands in the air, and students calling out, "Miss Roberts! I need your help!", but I have seen such a massive progression in their skills that the calls have now become, "Miss Roberts! Look at what I can do!".

The students have been amazing, and have really astonished us with their abilities.

Donna Roberts

Project Epilogue – BETT 2014

Here is a Press Release following the BETT 2014 Exhibition:

Presentation of work by the Swaminarayan School
BETT 2014, 25 January at Excel, Docklands

Under the Brunel University Partnership scheme, teachers and pupils at the Swaminarayan School, Neasden, have been supporting a pioneering Computing project, Literacy from Scratch. Designed originally for secondary pupils to develop their Computing skills, and presented by KS3 pupils last year at BETT 2013, the new pilot project targeted much younger pupils in Years 1 and 2, to see if they, too, could meet the demands of the Secretary of State, at KS1.

Pupils should be taught to:

- **understand what algorithms are**, how they are implemented as programs on digital devices, and that programs execute by following precise and unambiguous instructions
- **create and debug simple programs**
- **use logical reasoning to predict the behaviour of simple programs (Computing)**.

Could pupils aged only five and six years possibly do this?

Following weekly classroom support by Lawrence Williams, pupils in Ms Donna Roberts' Y1 and Mr Francis Naera's Y2 classes did, indeed, successfully meet all of the above demands, through the Literacy from Scratch programme.

Accordingly, Lawrence Williams invited the school to present this outstanding development to teachers at BETT 2014. The meeting, held under MirandaNet, was attended by teachers and academics in person, and virtually by many others watching abroad, via a web cast.

The Year 1 and Year 2 students were magnificent. Smartly dressed, confident, and articulate, they explained to the audience how they had worked on their Scratch projects: making their own stories; their own digital characters as Sprites; their own Backgrounds (in Paint); as well as moving between the three scenes; and adding both dialogue and animation. One Scratch file had a voice-over sound file in Gujarati. All were presented with a prestigious World Ecitizens Certificate by Dr Christina

Preston, Professor of Innovation at Bedfordshire University, and Chair of MirandaNet.

The teachers watching at BETT were amazed at the skills of the pupils, and described the work as "amazing", "inspiring", and "brilliant!"

My sincere thanks are due to the teachers, to the Year 1 and 2 pupils, who worked so well and to such good effect, and to Swaminarayan head teacher Mr Raja for kindly allowing the project to be developed at the school.

Further work is now planned to develop wider bi-lingual content for the project.

Note

1. Capital letters used, such as B for Background, or S for Sprites or Stage, denote the use of the term within the Scratch program.

4 Introducing Computing at Key Stage 2

Lawrence Williams with Ashlie Cox

This chapter focuses on developing Literacy from Scratch at KS2, through the work of a Brunel ITE student, Ashlie Cox, who developed this in her Year 5 and Year 6 classes while on placement. It is a different delivery model, therefore, but it proved to be very effective.

Here is the statutory guidance for KS2, and, in bold, how Literacy from Scratch helps to deliver it.

Pupils should be taught to:

- **design, write and debug programs that accomplish specific goals, including controlling or simulating physical systems; solve problems by decomposing them into smaller parts**
- **use sequence, selection, and repetition in programs; work with variables and various forms of input and output**
- **use logical reasoning to explain how some simple algorithms work and to detect and correct errors in algorithms and programs**
- understand computer networks, including the internet; how they can provide multiple services, such as the World Wide Web, and the opportunities they offer for communication and collaboration
- use search technologies effectively, appreciate how results are selected and ranked, and be discerning in evaluating digital content
- **select, use, and combine a variety of software (including internet services) on a range of digital devices to design and create a range**

of programs, systems, and content that accomplish given goals, including collecting, analysing, evaluating, and presenting data and information

- use technology safely, respectfully, and responsibly; recognise acceptable/unacceptable behaviour; identify a range of ways to report concerns about content and contact.

As part of her ITE Computer Science Specialism (now called Curriculum Enhancement) at Brunel University, one of the PGCE students, Ashlie Cox, developed the following series of three introductory lessons for Year 5 and Year 6.

This focus group project was conducted in a West London primary school with a total of 180 students. ICT is a large part of student learning across all ages, and is currently used to enhance a number of National Curriculum subjects. All students used in this project own a minimum of one computer in their family home, and use the computer a minimum of once daily.

Brunel project overview

This project was conducted over three planned lessons and was piloted using one Year 5 class (aged 9–10 years old) and one Year 6 class (aged 10–11 years old). Year 5 and Year 6 pupils were taught separately to allow independent learning. Previous learner experience of a computer programming application consisted of Flowol 4 only.

Lesson 1

Specific learning intention:

- I can navigate my way around Scratch.

Related success criteria:

- I can find the control to start a Scratch script.
- I can find add a new Sprite from a file.
- I can change the Stage (or Background).

Ashlie writes:

It was important for me to use the initial introduction to Scratch as an exploration lesson. I wanted to assess students' existing computer knowledge, and the speed at which students could learn Scratch, and to what degree. For this reason, I demonstrated story examples and what I thought were the important Scratch features, including Script, Stage, and Sprite. I shared some technical vocabulary with the students, and encouraged them to use the language throughout the lesson, especially when demonstrating completed work to peers.

The plenary was an imperative part of this lesson because it allowed me to assess students' learning, as well as to give students the opportunity for peer assessment. All students met the specific learning intention. Student assessment throughout and during plenary was integral to me as the teacher, for further lesson planning.

Lesson 2

Specific learning intention:

- I can begin to use a Sprite and Stage (or Background) to create a short story scene.

Related success criteria:

- I can control a Sprite using a Script.
- I can upload a complementary Stage.

Ashlie writes:

Lesson 2 began in the same way as lesson 1, and students were immediately excited to learn that we would be continuing with Scratch. I very briefly recapped the key features of Scratch, and instructed students to consider using their new skills to create a short story scene. I decided to allow the learners to choose their own story specifics, due to the varied interests in each group. I also thought this would provide a better overview of individual student knowledge of Scratch. I did, however, demonstrate my own story scene, and allowed students some time to discuss ideas amongst their peers.

The plenary was key to lesson 2. The majority of students had begun to create a good story scene and so it was both useful and inspiring for the students to assess peer work. Learners were engaged in both giving and receiving feedback. Although controversial in some areas of the National Curriculum, I encouraged students to adopt and develop ideas from each other for use in their own Scratch story scene, during plenary. All students met the specific lesson criteria in lesson 2.

Lesson 3

Specific learning intention:

● I can use audio in my short story scene.

Related success criteria:

● I can choose appropriate audio to complement my Scratch short story scene.

Ashlie writes:

Due to the speed that students had learnt to use Scratch, I decided to focus the final lesson on audio. Some students had already begun to enquire about audio files during lesson 2. Fortunately, this school was well equipped with ICT equipment, allowing a microphone per student. This may not always be the case, and so audio may be a feature to be integrated over a course of lessons to allow microphones to be shared. I began the lesson by demonstrating to the whole group how to record and upload an audio file into Scratch. Students grasped this with ease. I then placed the audio file into an example story scene, and demonstrated the importance of inserting the audio file into the script. The bulk of both focus groups had completed a short scene including some audio by the end of this lesson.

The final plenary was used to "show and tell" story scenes. Students moved around the ICT suite, considering peer work. We then evaluated the Scratch application as a whole class, commenting on both the positive and the negative aspects.

RECOMMENDATIONS FROM EXPERIENCE

Even though initially I decided to allow students the freedom and flexibility to create a scene theme of their choice, I feel it would be beneficial, given more time, to provide students with a more organised start to the project. By planning a beginning, middle, and end to a scene using a provided planning template, students may produce a better quality piece of work and furthermore this may give less able learners more structure. However, it would be crucial to dedicate a whole lesson to planning, especially for younger, or less able, students. As well as providing a planning template, it may be preferable to suggest story topics currently being taught in another area of the curriculum – for example, Egyptians or rivers.

I considered allowing students to work with partners during this short project, and although this particular focus group consisted of a majority of ICT literate students, there were a few pupils who did not grasp all of the concepts immediately. In my opinion, partnering these students would have hindered their learning because they were eventually able to independently produce a piece of computer programming work. Furthermore, the time set aside to assess peer work at the end of each lesson was invaluable to lower ability students. This vital time allowed them to become motivated, "steal" ideas, and learn about different features from peers. A future recommendation for Scratch, considering this area, would include "Cloud" access. This would then give students the opportunity to work in groups, but individually. This would also be especially beneficial in creating whole-class, whole-school or inter-school projects. An exciting prospect!

As this was a new application for the students, I believed it important to set achievable targets each lesson. I discussed the specific learning intentions at the start of the lesson, so that students were aware of exactly what was expected of them. Since working with this focus group, I have learnt the importance of setting differentiated success criteria. Some students were able to meet the lesson objective immediately and so I verbally stretched them. It would be preferable to demonstrate the extension work from the beginning of the lesson. Providing the students with levelled success criteria would be idyllic.

A particular concern during this focus group project included time. Consequently, students decided to use the ICT suite during lunch break to complete their story scenes. Much to my surprise, this included the lower ability learners. I would recommend a minimum of a term to complete a high-quality story, taking advantage of all the features of Scratch for KS2 learners. Given more time overall, I would dedicate a larger portion of each lesson to peer assessment. Using tools such as PMIQ charts would not only benefit student Scratch projects, but also provide time for further skills development, such as Speaking and Listening (EN1). It was important for the success of student projects to allow time each lesson for peer discussion. Sharing and borrowing ideas from each other was crucial in the progression of pupil learning outcomes.

Due to the nature and structure of this project, I was able to assess students throughout the lesson. On reflection, I would provide clear guidelines to the LSA for assessment, to allow me to work with, and provide more in-depth Scratch knowledge to, particular students. This would further benefit the students, and I would still be able to check learner progress for further planning during plenary.

Ashlie's work, including the pupils' learning outcomes, is posted on www.literacyfromscratch.org.uk.

5   Introducing Computing at Key Stage 3

Lawrence Williams with Nick Mayne

As more demanding Computing skills are developed at Key Stage 3, Literacy from Scratch inevitably meets fewer of these additional targets. Nonetheless, it has proved very valuable for encouraging Year 8 pupils to work at developing their enthusiasm for Computing, and it also helps to develop the following Key Stage 3 elements:

- understand how instructions are stored and executed within a computer system; understand how data of various types (including text, sounds, and pictures) can be represented and manipulated digitally, in the form of binary digits
- undertake creative projects that involve selecting, using, and combining multiple applications, preferably across a range of devices, to achieve challenging goals, including collecting and analysing data and meeting the needs of known users.

And it is fun!

Using "Scratch" to support literacy development: a collaboration between Brunel University (Education) and Bishop Ramsey C of E School, Ruislip

These are the participants in the original pilot project, which led to the further developments that have been outlined in the preceding two chapters.

Brunel University's Education Department has an Erasmus Bilateral Agreement with The Charles University in Prague. As part of this new collaboration, educational projects are currently being developed between Czech schools and UK schools, using ICT tools, especially the development of computer programming.

World Ecitizens is an international web site created by teachers to give students a "voice", by publishing their learning outcomes.

MirandaNet is a leading online community of teachers, dedicated to sharing best educational ICT practice at an international level.

Scratch 1.4 is an elementary computer programming language, developed at MIT.

Technical note: While version 2.0 is more powerful, it is cloud-based, and this gives rise to potential access problems for pupils, especially at KS1 and KS2.

Year 8 Scratch pilot project: aims at Bishop Ramsey School

● To develop computer programming skills using Scratch
● To develop narrative skills using Scratch
● To publish student learning outcomes (on World Ecitizens) and a project report for teachers (on MirandaNet) and Literacy from Scratch web sites
● To explore new ways of collaborating with Brunel University

Objective

Students in Year 8 ICT lessons will explore the use of Scratch to create a piece of narrative work, by creating about ten linked scenes (called Backgrounds). Characters will then be added to the scenes, and animated, and soundtracks may also be added. This work may be linked to English, Music, and Art lessons. Students may work alone or in pairs.

Method

Introductory lessons will be given to Year 8 students by Lawrence Williams, Teaching Fellow at Brunel. The project will be explained to staff and pupils, and the tasks will be introduced in these lessons. Support from the university will be maintained through weekly visits.

Assessment

Following the lesson development, the stories will be assessed:

- as successful narrative work (narrative structure, development of characters, use of dialogue, and description)
- as effective (efficient) computer programming
- for cross-curricular elements, such as art work (developing pupils' own sprites and background scenes), and music (development of soundtracks in music lessons, or as homework).

This plan was highly successful. In February 2013, four pupils from Year 8 in the Bishop Ramsey School were invited to present their lovely stories to an academic audience at the BETT 2013 Exhibition in London, where they were joined by Dr Miroslava Černochová from Charles University in Prague. (See Miroslava's Chapter 2, which underpins the pedagogy behind the project.)

Subsequently, all the teaching materials developed at the school were posted on the www.literacyfromscratch.org.uk web site.

Project outline

This is probably a full term's work, based on a weekly 45-minute lesson.

Note:
There are free videos on the Scratch web site showing how to do each of the following activities.

First steps

Start with a story (working with your English Department?), and then, over a series of lessons, perhaps nine or ten, you can:

1. Use the Paint Editor within the Scratch program to create your own characters, called Sprites. You can borrow (or "import") Sprites from within the Scratch program itself, but it is far more fun, and more fulfilling, to create your own.
2. Use the Paint Editor within the Scratch program to create three or more different Backgrounds (the three or more scenes for your story). The more characters and scenes you have, however, the more difficult it is to manage the timings later. Adjust this aspect according to the age and ability of the pupils.

   It is a good idea to keep Backgrounds very simple – just a half page of colour wash (use the Fill button) of blue for the sky, green for grass, yellow for a sandy beach, etc. This has two advantages:

   a. It saves time, and pupils are not caught up in extensive art work, though you may want this to happen in the Art Department!
   b. It allows the Sprites/characters to be seen against the Background. Complex Backgrounds obscure the characters. If there is time, pupils can later add more detail. When they know where their characters are placed, for example, they may add a tree, or clouds, or a lamp post, if there is space available on the page. This is a useful and creative Extension Activity.

3. Add the dialogue for the characters.
4. Add animations.
5. Check the timings.
6. Add further details, redesigning the Sprites; adding detail to the Backgrounds; add sound files for special effects; add voice-over commentaries; add music files.

Further, extensive support materials can be found on the Literacy from Scratch web site, including examples of good practice created by pupils and teachers. These can be downloaded, deconstructed, and shown to classes. The project model is basically the same as that described in more detail in Chapter 3. The only difference is that, at secondary level, Computing teachers may need to liaise with their English Department colleagues, in order for them to work with appropriate narrative material. At primary level, this is much easier to manage, of course, as the ICT/Computing teacher and the English teacher are the same person. At secondary level, there are also possibilities for the Computing teacher to work with the school Music Department, to provide suitable musical soundtracks for the narratives. Media Studies might also be interested in getting involved, as the stories rapidly, and inevitably, become multi-media.

Teacher comments

> *The "Literacy from Scratch" project has helped all of my students in Year 8 (aged 12 to 13) to develop not only their literacy skills, but also their understanding of computer programming.*
>
> *It is refreshing to see students so engaged in a project that involves programming. Some pupils stayed through their break times to work on their projects, even those who found it difficult at times!*
>
> *I have been impressed with how much this project has spanned many subjects across the curriculum.*
>
> *We plan to work more closely with other Departments next year. These will include ICT/CS teachers, English, Music, and Art teachers.*
>
> *Nick Mayne, Bishop Ramsey School*

Pupil evaluation

> *I have really enjoyed doing this Scratch project, and I feel that it has really helped with learning basic skills that I can apply elsewhere. I think what went well was the fact that the teaching was impressive, and the examples inspired me to do something differently. I also think the fact that we had plenty of time was good, as it meant my work wasn't rushed, and I had time to think about every detail of my project. Another good thing that went well was the fact we could be imaginative, and we didn't have to stick to a story, you could have any twist and turn, and it was your original story. One other thing that went really well was that your partner checked the spelling. I myself am not great at spelling, and so this helped me to put commas and full stops in the right places. The last thing that went well was the fact that we could paint our own characters, and that we didn't have to use the Sprites on Scratch. This was good because you could be imaginative and draw characters of all different kinds.*

I didn't particularly enjoy using Scratch itself, as I am not the most technical person, but I did enjoy planning the story with my partner, and choosing which idea worked best. I also really enjoyed designing my own characters and recording my own sounds. The fact we could see other projects was really good to watch as it made me think about how mine could be better. The main thing I have learnt on the Scratch project is that you don't want to have massive text bubbles for your characters to say, as this is boring for the audience, but you do want to engage them in the story and make it seem like they are actually there. I have also learnt that you have to involve the audience by asking them rhetorical questions, to make them feel that they are part of the story, and I have learnt that you have to have some humour in it as well, in order to catch the audience's attention.

To be a good storyteller you have to have a climax in the story where the characters have some sort of problem, and it has to be resolved. I also think that the characters have to have different per-sonalities, and that there has to be a "Baddy" in the story. To be a good storyteller, you also have to make sure that everything is spelled correctly so that the viewers have a more enjoyable read. I have also learnt the skill of copying and pasting characters from the internet onto Scratch and altering the Backgrounds on them. The main skills I learnt have to be the fact that you have to line up the computer pro-gramme timings, so that everything slots together perfectly!

I think a great deal has been learned here.

Have a look at the web site for more detailed lesson plans, cross-curricular teaching ideas, and some lovely work by some very talented pupils.

Literacy from Scratch: some thoughts on pedagogy

Pedagogical approaches in London and Prague

While the Literacy from Scratch project is a joint international venture, it is clear that there are differences emerging between the approaches to the classroom use of Scratch for developing creative narrative work in the two countries:

In London, the work undertaken in the classroom is being driven by a teacher of English, and the project is therefore seen from a Literacy viewpoint. The Planning Sheet grids are completed in words, for example.

In Prague, by contrast, the same project is being driven by a school in which art and creativity are central, and so the classwork developed is seen largely from an artistic viewpoint. This includes the Planning Sheets, which are completed using pupils' own images. Examples are posted on this web site: www.literacyfromscratch.org.uk.

Both countries use storyboarding techniques, therefore, but in two very different ways.

Both countries agree, however, that these two approaches need to be supported and developed in the future, by the addition of music sound files (WAV and MPEG) created in the classroom by pupils, which can provide background, atmospheric accompaniment to parts of their unfolding narratives.

Further work is being developed using voice-over sound files for the Sprites, when they are speaking or thinking.

In London, the work is being taken further across the curriculum: into maths, science, history and geography – anywhere in which narrative lines can be used to develop pupil learning. A new web section is being added to illustrate this cross-curricular use of Scratch.

In Prague, the activity is also being further developed across the curriculum, from literacy to communicate, into language and ICT education.

Most important

The most important practical aspect of learning how to use Scratch has, in both countries, been to deconstruct existing examples of projects – that is, to look at successful coding, and to learn from these examples how to solve problems. In Prague, files sent from the UK were used both as a stimulus for creativity and as examples from which Czech pupils could learn details of successful coding practice. The ICT student teacher (ITE) explained to the ICT and language teachers how their pupils would work and developed study materials (also on the web site: www.literacyfromscratch.org.uk) for the project. In this way, experienced teachers were able to learn from younger student teachers how to work in Scratch.

At Brunel University, the workshop plenary sessions in which trainee student teachers shared their work with each other proved to be the most valuable parts of the workshop sessions. There were shared solutions to coding problems, and the stimulus of seeing the creative ideas of others also resulted in further creative ideas. The plenary sessions were steadily increased in length, as the project developed.

Future developments

Two developments are clearly necessary, one regarding the range of literacy content, the other regarding the computing content:

1. The narrative aspects of this work need to be developed much more fully. At present, the results are very good examples of what might be termed drama or film scripts, but with little sustained narrative line. Nor is there presently scope for much descriptive writing, because the Sprites and Backgrounds are clearly visible, and do not therefore need to be described. This weakness also stems from the fact that the structure is provided by the setting out of the story in separate scenes, using the Backgrounds. We plan to explore how to strengthen these elements over the coming few terms.
2. The range of computer coding elements used (Motion, Looks, Sound, and Control) is also limited. We plan to find ways of developing Sensing, Operators, and Variables, as the next step.
   One way forward will be through the creation of:

   a. Branching Stories (If, Then, Else, And, Or, Not) and using a wider range of coding skills
   b. Interactive Stories, in which pupils can use the Sensing coding, as well as interacting with the teaching material presented on the interactive White Board.

This work is currently being developed at Brunel University by ITE student teachers as part of their Curriculum Enhancement programme. At the time of writing, progress in both the literacy and the coding aspects is good.

Developments in teacher training using Literacy from Scratch are also being undertaken in Italy, at the University of Torino. See: http://t4t.di.unito.it/T4T2013.html.

Developments in Primary Art within the project are being further developed at Korunavachni School, and at Charles University, Prague.

All of the new work will be posted on the Literacy from Scratch web site: www.literacyfromscratch.org.uk.

We are also developing the World Ecitizens web site, to house new Scratch projects which also incorporate an international dimension. The first of these is the creation of Scratch files in more than one language. For example, files in English have already been translated into Italian and Russian, and some of the primary school files from Swaminarayan have had Gujarati voice-over sound files added, to make them bi-lingual.

This work will be housed at the World Ecitizens web site: www.world ecitizens.net/literacy-from-scratch/.

It is clear that Computing in schools is developing rapidly, both in the UK and abroad, with support materials becoming available from many sources. Many countries are looking at the UK Computing curriculum to see how this work progresses.

Final thoughts

- Literacy from Scratch is an ideal way of starting the development of work in Computing because the focus of the pupil is on the actual story-telling, rather than on abstract coding. Pupils want the coding to work, to ensure that their story will unfold properly, and because they want their characters to speak and move at the correct moment, and in the correct position.
- The project demands collaborative, creative, and cross-curricular work. This is essential if the narrative, the art work, the music, and the computing skills are to be completed and integrated successfully. It is ideal for developing cross-curricular project work at primary level, as we saw at Swaminarayan School (Chapter 3) and for starting meaningful cross-departmental collaboration at secondary level.
- Scratch stories in more than one language, and stories from different cultures, can be a powerful support for multi-cultural awareness.
- Above all, it is fun, and positively engages pupils of all ages, from age 5 to 13.

6 Communications and networks

Mark Dorling

Introduction

Networking is a completely new topic for most schools. It is, nonetheless, relatively easy to introduce the required material to pupils. This can be accomplished "off computer", or "unplugged", as a series of practical, lively, and engaging activities.

The Programmes of Study specify that children need to:

- understand computer networks, including the internet; how they can provide multiple services, such as the World Wide Web, and the opportunities they offer for communication and collaboration
- use search technologies effectively, appreciate how results are selected and ranked, and be discerning in evaluating digital content.

Some teachers were surprised by the inclusion of this at primary level, but there are many ways of quite easily introducing these concepts to children as young as seven years of age, using the lesson suggestions which follow.

Many of these activities do not need computer access, but can be developed through discussion and kinaesthetic activities.

Lesson 1

What is the difference between the World Wide Web and the internet?

We need to start with some key concepts:

A computer network: a group of computers connected together wirelessly or by wires.

A server: a piece of hardware or software that responds to requests from client computers across a computer network to provide a network service. In this respect, it is a bit like a library, where people ask for books to borrow and are served by a librarian.

A client: a piece of computer hardware or software that accesses a service made available by a server. It is therefore more like the person who actually visits the library.

The internet: an interconnected network of computer networks.

The World Wide Web: more commonly known as the web. When we use a web browser, we use the abbreviation "www." in the address bar. The World Wide Web is the system of interlinked documents (like library books) stored on servers. These digital artefacts are most commonly accessed via a web browser – for example, Google Chrome, Microsoft Internet Explorer, or Mozilla Firefox.

Plan

Begin the lesson by asking the children if they have ever been to a library? Most of the children will reply "yes". Ask them in pairs or small groups to list all the different services they can obtain in the library and the types of materials that are available – for example, books, magazines, newspapers, CDs, videos, DVDs, advice about local events.

Young children may struggle with the services that are also available – for example, newspapers, books, video, audio (World Wide Web), and community chat areas (VOIP), etc.

Then ask the children: "If I were to move all the books from the library and move them to another building, where is the library?" If the child believes that the actual building is the library, then it will not have moved. However, if a child believes that the items and services within the building are what make a library then it will have moved.

With this discussion in mind, you are able to consider how the library system works and relate this back to the difference between the internet and World Wide Web. Begin this teaching by asking the children how they borrow a book from the library. Ask them to describe the process (see Figure 6.1).

Challenge the children by asking them what happens if they want an item from the library that is not actually in stock, or is not stocked at all in their particular library. Some children will be aware of the process – that is, one library will look for the item by searching for it at neighbouring libraries. When the book is found to be in stock, it is requested and transported by van to the requesting library, and the library user is then informed that the book is ready for collection. Ask the children how long they think this process takes. If they don't know, encourage them to take a visit to the library to find out!

Model the process on the classroom white board where one library may request items from many libraries; the children could draw a diagram (see Figure 6.2). Ask the children what happens if one of those other libraries receives a request from a user for an item that is not stocked. The children will say that they will also search and request the item from other libraries. The children should then add links between all the libraries showing how the items can flow between the libraries.

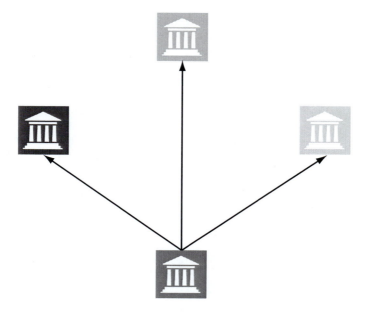

Figure 6.1 Choosing a book.

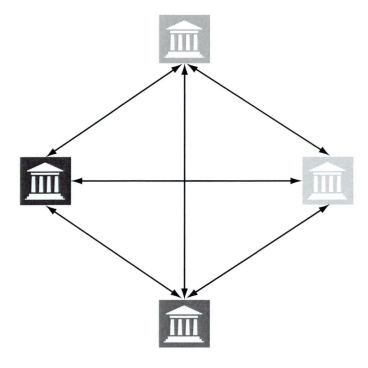

Figure 6.2 Searching other libraries.

To help the children to grasp the ideas above, you can perform a human internet activity. Begin the activity by asking the children what the word "server" means. The children will probably liken it to a "servant" or assistant – that is, someone who brings you things – or a lunchtime supervisor, who helps to manage the food in the lunch hall.

Split the class into small groups and give each group a name (e.g. server 1). Distribute the children in the classroom or school hall. Give each group of children a pile of books from the school library and place them on a table. Create a set of instruction cards that request a particular book from a particular group of children (i.e. a server). The table is the server, the books are the documents being transported on the internet, and the children fetch and return the books for the client. Then give the children instructions: each child in the group takes it in turn to fetch and return their item listed on the card. To prevent the items simply swapping tables, explain to the children that they can only borrow a certain number of items at any one time. Therefore, the child to request (collect) the item has to return it to the original server before the group requests the next book.

To make this game more fun, you can turn it into a quiz. When the item has been collected, you can ask the children for a specific piece of information, such as the second word, third paragraph, page 72 (which sets up the next lesson's activity nicely on finding information on a page). When you put many of these clues together, you uncover a secret message! This activity can be extended to cover a digital literacy concept of ownership of digital artefacts by asking the children to record the date, time, and server details that the clues were taken from. By asking the children previously to return the items when finished, you can do this activity as a race. But check health and safety issues first!

After completing the activity, refer the children back to the question about the books in the library. The children will be more likely to now say that the items in the library are what make a library. This provides you with the opportunity to relate this understanding to the documents on the internet being the World Wide Web, with the library being the computer, the vans being the system for transferring the documents between libraries as the network, with the digital artefacts in the libraries being the World Wide Web.

If the children were able to come up with services available in the library, it is worth discussing with them that they are not the items (i.e. books, audio CDs etc.), but stand-alone services also offered by the library. Therefore, when using the internet, you can use things such as VOIP (e.g. Skype and email), which work through the internet but are not the World Wide Web.

This lesson has provided a foundation for learning about the structure of the internet, and how the World Wide Web actually works.

Lesson 2

Searching the World Wide Web

We need to start with some key concepts:

Search engine: a program that searches for and identifies items in a database that correspond to keywords specified by the user, used especially for finding particular web pages on the internet.

Web crawler: also known as a web spider, these are used by search engines. They visit a list of URLs (called seeds). The web crawler updates the web content, including all the hyperlinks in the web page, and adds them to a list of web pages to visit (called crawler frontier), and these are then visited. This is also important for the Search Engine Page Ranking, which is covered in later lessons.

Plan

Begin the lesson by recapping on what they learnt last lesson, reviewing what the following words mean, and see if they can remember the difference between the internet and the World Wide Web:

- Internet
- World Wide Web
- Server
- Client

Ask the children what things they consider when choosing a book from the library. The teacher will probably be given the following answers:

- Title
- Blurb
- Author
- Size of the book
- Date published
- Design or illustration of the cover

Encourage the children to do a search using one of the well-known search engines. Ask them to consider which search result they will pick. Children will usually tell the teacher that they will go for the top links without reading the blurb about the web page, which is surprising as most children consider the blurb on a book before using it.

Ask the children to see if they can relate the criteria they use when selecting a book to the results from the search engine.

On completion of this activity, there is an opportunity to help the children relate the documents on the internet (i.e. World Wide Web) to the books in the library. Therefore, rather than the search engine being the World Wide Web, they will recognise that it is a program for searching the digital artefacts stored on servers connected to the internet, which we call the World Wide Web.

If the children are still struggling with the understanding of the role of the search engine, you can take the children for a school trip to the local library where they can use the computer in the library to search for a particular item or book. Using the information it provides (i.e. building, floor, category, aisle, shelf number), the children can fetch the item they were looking for.

To extend the children, and to encourage them to become more efficient with their searches and understand how a web crawler works, the children should be given a web site link and a set of questions relating to the web page. The questions relate to particular keywords on a web page (this is a great opportunity for some cross-curricular work). The questions could be to find particular keywords or the number of times a keyword appears on a web page, or the information contained in a sentence where that keyword is located.

The first few questions ask the children to search for the keywords manually, which takes them quite some time – the children have to scroll down the page looking for the answers. Then encourage the children to look through the menu tabs in the web browser of choice to identify a relevant tool (i.e. Edit > Find).

Ask the children to search for the second five questions, but this time using the "Find" tool within the web browser. Also ask the children to find and list all the hyperlinks on the web page and their Uniform Resource Locator (URL).

It is important for the teacher during the plenary session to help children to evaluate the activities they have performed, including how they performed the role of the web crawler, as this will provide them with a useful foundation for how search results are selected and the order (rank) in which they appear in the results list in later lessons.

This lesson can also provide the class teacher with the opportunity to visit validity and trustworthiness of a web page, including consideration of fact, opinion, and bias. For resources on how to teach this, we would recommend that you visit the Digital Schoolhouse web site: www.resources.digitalschoolhouse.org.uk/digital-literacy-a-esafety/105-dsh-online-epassport-primary.

Lesson 3

How a search engine selects web pages and an introduction to Boolean logic

We need to start with some key concepts:

Boolean searches: Boolean searches allow a user to combine words and phrases using connective words (otherwise known as Boolean operators), such as AND, OR, and NOT, when asking questions of the data. The purpose of using these Boolean operators can be to limit (narrow), widen (broaden), or define your search.

Venn diagram: Venn diagrams comprise two or more overlapping circles, which will be the case for our internet searches. The interior of the overlapping circle represents the elements of the set, while the exterior parts of the circles represent elements that are not members of the set.

Plan

Begin this lesson by giving each child a card with a screen shot of a web page on each card. If you are making your own, try to cover a range of cross-curricular subjects and topics. In particular, try and include web sites where the same words can be used in different contexts – for example, "war" could mean a BBC site covering a conflict somewhere in the world, or the game "World War 2", or the "Warcraft" game. This is particularly important when covering Boolean searches when narrowing down or broadening the search criteria.

The teacher explains that the classroom is the internet. The digital artefacts (i.e. web pages) are held on a server. Each child is a server storing multiple web pages (i.e. each child has multiple cards). The children are given a list of possible keywords that the teacher might search for during the activity. Like the last lesson, the children perform the role of a web crawler, looking through their digital artefacts for the keywords. To reinforce the role of the server, when the teacher does a search (i.e. asks a question), the teacher details only the keyword criterion (e.g. Romans). The answer to whether or not the web page contains that keyword and meets the criteria is going to be either "yes" or "no". If the child is holding a card (i.e. the server contains a web page) that meets the search criteria, then they as the server have something to "offer", so they would stand up holding the card(s). If the child's card does not meet the criteria, they should remain seated and not offer their card(s). The children will learn more about how the search engine uses the data from the web crawler to order the search results in the next lesson.

Boolean searches can be integrated into the activity by asking the children how we can make the process of doing multiple searches more efficient by removing the web pages that they do not want from the search results. The children will come up with the suggestion to join the searches together. This provides key questioning opportunities to identify connective words they use in Literacy – for example, AND, OR, and NOT – which could be used to join these searches. The children should have the opportunity to perform this learning using the server and web page activity previously described.

To conclude, the learning on Boolean searches asks children to consider how the use of AND, OR, and NOT affects the number of search results. If necessary, kinaesthetic learning where the children can count the number of "yes" and "no" answers for each question to reinforce their observations of:

- AND reduces (narrows) the number of children; and
- OR increases (expands) the number of children.

An engaging way to introduce the concept and assess the children's understanding of Boolean logic is to search for the criteria "Boy AND Girl"! This generates some debate in the class when they realise that you cannot be both a boy and a girl. The children will then have more ownership of how to rephrase the question using a different connective (i.e. OR), so that they are in fact standing in the right place.

This activity should be extended to cover the study of Venn diagrams and use of a search engine. You can either base the development of the Venn diagrams on the results from the questions asked in the Human Search Engine activity or one search engine where Boolean operators are used. For example, you can base it on human physical features as the search criteria – for example, "boys" and "brown hair" (see Figure 6.3) or another search on "girls" and "glasses".

Alternatively, this could be based on the use of Boolean operators with a recommended maximum of three search criteria on the internet using a search engine. The cross over between the circles represents the AND, with the total of both the respective circles and the cross-over representing the OR.

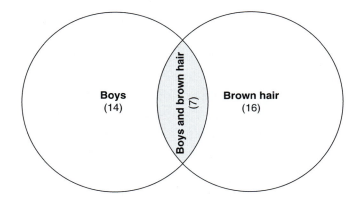

Figure 6.3 Boolean searches.

You can also help children to understand how Boolean logic can make web searches more efficient. Children can model searches and results using both a Venn diagram and a web browser to help them understand how the structure of the query affects (theoretically) the number of results. For example, searching for a combination of, and all, the three keywords: "bicycles", "holidays" and "Mongolia" and recording the results in a Venn diagram (see Figure 6.4). However, as a general rule of thumb, most search engines will process operators from left to right.

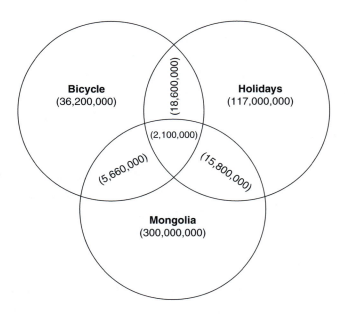

Figure 6.4 Boolean operators.

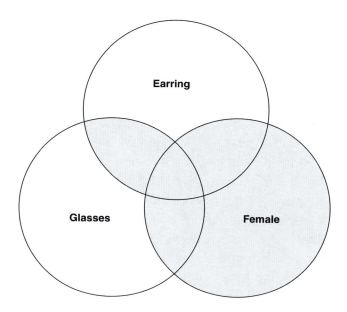

Figure 6.5 Earring AND glasses OR female.

To extend the children, the class teacher can combine Boolean operators AND and OR into the same query. A nice assessment of the learning activity is to ask the children to work on sets by colouring in the Venn diagram to show the expected search results based on the kinaesthetic learning activity from earlier in the lesson. For example, see Figure 6.5.

On completing these two activities, children will have an understanding both of how the pages are selected, including an introduction to Boolean logic, and of how to apply this understanding to improve their use of search engines by using keyword search criteria and Boolean logic to narrow or broaden search results.

Lesson 4

How search engines rank the web pages into an order

Plan

Begin this lesson by consolidating the role of the search engine – that is, it is a computer program that provides a list of the web pages in which the search criteria entered by the user appear in a web page, in the results list.

Show the children a page of search results from a popular search engine. Ask the children how they think the search engine orders these search results. Most children will say that they think it is based on which web pages are most popular. This creates an excellent PHSE study opportunity to have a discussion around what is "popularity". Focus your key questioning around the fact that we are all part of a number of small social groups of friends, each of which is relatively small.

Ask the children to think about how their social groups differ from their friends' – for example, through extra-curricular clubs. So in effect they are connected to people in other friendship groups they do not know via friends that they have in common; it is a nice idea to ask the children to identify friends that they have in common. Explain that this is known as small-world theory or six degrees of separation. There are some nice video clips available advertising a communications provider on the World Wide Web called "Three degrees of Kevin Bacon". Kevin Bacon is a famous Hollywood actor who scientists have found most other actors and actresses are connected to, and it is illustrated in these adverts.

It is helpful for future learning to remind the children that each social group is a network, and the interconnecting network is how we describe the internet.

The class teacher can develop this learning in a digital literacy direction by asking the children to list some of the web sites they have heard about or use that enable people to connect with one another and model their social groups (e.g. Facebook or LinkedIn). Ask children to consider both the advantages and disadvantages of such web sites. Ask the children whether they think that Kevin Bacon is the most popular actor. The answer will most likely be "no", but we are talking about him because he is very well connected with other people due to the range of films he has been in and the actors/actresses he has worked with.

Explain to the children that, like in human networks, there is no central authority that governs which web pages should be connected to which, so therefore there is no one way of finding the web page you need. In the next activity, children will learn how search engines (e.g. Google) use this idea of small-world theory when ranking the search results into an order.

Now that the children have a basic understanding of how the search engine selects results and understands what is meant by popularity, the Google Page activity, created by Doug Aberdeen, teaches children how the Google Page Ranking System actually works, through a lovely kinaesthetic learning activity.

The class teacher pins up screen shots of web pages around the room. Each web page has hyperlinks marked on it with a number. The children start at any web page they like the look of. They roll the dice and move to the new web page that the number on the dice corresponds to. After a dozen or so rolls of the dice, the children will notice that they will generally appear to move between the same web pages. Ask the children why they think this is so. Encourage the children to focus on the work earlier in the lesson on "popularity" and how the hyperlinks (connections) between web pages make a web page more popular. If the children struggle to make the connection between this learning, then encourage them to examine the hyperlinks (connections) between the web pages – considering which ones appear the most.

Essentially, the algorithm that powers the computer program uses the data from the web crawler to work out which web pages are the most popular and then it returns these at the top of the list of results that it delivers to you.

In the case of Doug Aberdeen's activity, the more stars a web page has, the higher the number of hyperlinks that are directed to the web page. For example, web page A and web page B are both about vampires. If ten other web pages link to web page A and five other web pages link to web page B, a search for "vampires" will return web page A at the top of the list of results. Therefore, a web page that has more pages linking to it will appear higher on the search results list; unless one of the hyperlinks directing to web page B had a much higher page rank value (e.g. BBC or similar sized organisation), which in effect means that each hyperlink (connection) is weighted. The children can understand this concept by likening it to the "popularity" discussion earlier, by asking whether they think that if the most popular child in the school became their friend, would this raise their "popularity" in school?

On completing these activities with a digital literacy focus, children develop an understanding of both how the internet is structured and how the Google Page Rank works. It provides an excellent foundation for learning about data transmission between digital computers over networks, including an introduction to binary, internet protocol (IP), Packet Switching, and how computers transfer data in binary.

Class teacher feedback

The children from the school had a wonderfully "mind-expanding" day. Our topic of study was "The World and travel" this term so we chose the day on the World Wide Web and discovered how information travels on the internet around the world. Mr Dorling related each area of computer science to simple analogies that the primary aged children could relate to, such as postcodes for IP addresses. The knack the project has is getting the children to wrestle with complicated concepts while they think they are "playing around" in games about computers or on the computers themselves, which is truly phenomenal. The children's understanding increases exponentially and each child is challenged and motivated throughout the day.

(Head teacher and OFSTED inspector)

Primary school children's feedback

I learnt about the internet and how it works. I felt very excited because I was looking forward to that day. I have learnt a lot during the day. I also really enjoyed learning about how a search engine works. Finally, I would like to say that I really enjoyed my day at Digital Schoolhouse and I hope I will come here again some time.

(Aged 10)

I really liked learning about the internet and how it works. I thought that the activities and games were really fun and it made us think hard about what we were learning. I found understanding how the internet works and relating it to how the four libraries/servers work together to give me the documents I want on the internet. I look forward to coming back and learning some more about the internet.

(Aged 9)

7 Gaming and Computing

*Nic Crowe and
Rosie Hussain*

Defending the dark arts

Digital play in the classroom

"The problem with wizards is that they are basically weak and not very skilled with any weapons other than magic. Orcs are tough, have well hard armour and lots of big weapons. So the trick is to design your dungeon with lots of bits that Orcs can't get through. So I put in traps to kill them, gaps – cuz Orcs can't jump – and narrow passages that they have ta squeeze through." It's Wednesday afternoon, and though it feels a little like I am in Middle Earth, I am actually paying another visit to the computer and science club. Games programming seems to be the order of the day. All around me, pupils are transfixed to a range of digital constructions at varying stages of completion. At the far end, two girls are tweaking an insect-like robotic model that creeps around a somewhat sparse digital landscape on six legs. Next to them, a group of boys noisily put the finishing touches to a lush jungle – a level for a maze game designed on "Blender 3D". I am getting a lesson on repelling orcs from Lee, Tif and Vik, three Year 10 students who have been working on their story using the quest editor option built into the fantasy game "Darkstone". *"I am about to run a test,"* Lee tells me excitedly, *"wanna see?"* We gather around the screen. Vik's wizard appears in the middle of the dungeon and begins

to explore his dark and dank surroundings. Suddenly a war band of Orcs burst through the walls at the far end. Vik grins gleefully at Lee as he unleashes a volley of spells cutting down two of his attackers. Unperturbed the remaining Orcs continue to advance. Out of spells, Vik turns tail and flees, only to be stopped by a large ravine cutting off his escape. He mutters something intelligible under his breath. "You're not going to make that," warns Tif, at the exact same moment that Vik launches from the edge of the ravine and hurtles to his doom on the floor below. "Man that was hard," moans Vik turning to Lee, "you made it too difficult". "Nah," grins Lee, "you just didn't do it right!"

(Field Diary entry)

Toil and trouble

These are uncertain times for wizards – digital wizards in particular! The computing landscape of schools is changing once again as it begins to accommodate (or perhaps more correctly re-accommodate) Computer Science alongside its ICT curriculum. Since the 1980s, when computers were first launched into schools, there has been an almost continuous introduction of "new" technology-driven initiatives that have often been funded through wider government agendas. Yet in many ways the partnership between Technology and Education has remained a troubled one. New Labour placed the emergent digital technologies firmly at the centre of their education strategy in the early noughties. But despite the then Secretary of State for Education Charles Clarke's assertion that it "has the potential to revolutionise the way we teach and the way we learn ... and to bring high quality accessible learning to everyone – so that every learner can achieve his or her potential" (Department for Education and Skills, 2003, p. 1) arguably in many cases "money has been spent on ICT on the basis of faith or blind belief in its vocational (and sometimes pedagogical) value, rather than on any basis of evidence" (Wellington, 2005, p. 28). However, digital resources are now utilised by almost half of all primary pupils on a weekly basis (BECTA, 2009) and the use of digital technology both in school and in the home is seen by many as an integral and fundamental aspect of childhood (Byron, 2010).

But for many educationalists, not all technology is the same. The educational role of the popular technologies – digital games, phones, and social media, for example – has continuously generated stormy debate. Supporters of these digital platforms (see Gee, 2007; McAlister, 2009;

Crowe, 2013) criticise the teaching profession for their reluctance to embrace new or unfamiliar technology. Conversely, the "denouncers" rigorously maintain that by introducing these "populist" platforms into the classroom, teachers forgo real learning in favour of little more than "edutainment" (see Postman, 1985; Greenwald & Rosner, 2003; Wellington 2005). However, contemporary experiences are an important aspect of effective learning (Friere, 1985) and research has identified how familiar technologies can improve motivation and confidence (Valentine *et al.*, 2005). Gee (2003) mischievously suggests that, compared to the somewhat dry and ineffective learning experiences offered by many traditional e-based approaches, popular technology is fun and immersive. Although it might be simple to sideline these platforms as a lazy and un-scholastic form of learning, to do so would be to miss out on exciting ways to engage children (Crowe & Flynn, 2013).

In this chapter, we want briefly to consider the relationship between popular digital technology and education practice in the hope that it will serve as an inspiration to try new things in the Computing classroom. We are not sure that Wellington's earlier pessimism is now the case. There is growing evidence that learning benefits arise from the use of a range of digital technologies (Underwood, 2009) and, as Livingstone (2012) points out, it would be excessively pessimistic to determine that no benefits can be gained through using new technology in education. There is an emergent body of work – for example, MIT (in the US) and Futurelab (here in the UK) – that demonstrates an education dimension to popular technology. As we have suggested elsewhere (Crowe, 2013), when utilised properly – to enrich, inspire, and transform learning – popular digital platforms are being increasingly adopted by teachers to facilitate good learning (Simpson *et al.*, 2011).

Yet, despite this evidence and optimism, there is also reluctance on the part of many educational professionals to enter the digital dungeon, as one young primary school teacher explains:

> *I know that we need to look at new ways of keeping the children engaged, but computer games and the like are just one step too far. No one teaches you about them when you are training, the Head (Teacher) and parents are suspicious of anything new, so when you are just starting out you just don't have the confidence. I guess when you have been teaching for a bit you might try something different, but most experienced teachers I know stick to the tried and tested*

> *methods that they know work.... School is not the place to stick your neck out I suppose, you just need to get the work done.*
>
> *(Tammi)*

Different reasons can be ascribed to the attitudes teachers may have towards the introduction of "new" technologies to their practices. As Tammi shows us, this could range from a lack of confidence about using the technology itself, to the need to complete strict curriculum requirements within specified times, or a fear of encountering popular prejudices from parents and school management. Perhaps it is not surprising then that many teachers will opt for what they deem as the trusted way of delivering the curriculum.

For technology to be an effective learning tool, teachers have to create a strategy or pedagogy to make it work in *their* classroom. In order to do this, they must first know how to utilise the complete range of technologies at their disposal, whilst also acquiring a complex understanding of how to ensure that it is educationally appropriate for the pupils (Leask, 2001). In other words, the teacher's attitude to, and their relationship with, technology has a direct effect on the way he or she chooses to use it in the classroom. Unfamiliar or "risky" technology is often rejected because it is not seen as being a legitimate tool for learning, regardless of whether it can be an effective means of engagement.

Arguably, our "problem" with popular technology lies with us, the educator, rather than with the technology itself:

> *I asked Sir if we could use the game "Portal" in science as Mr Dickens' class had been using it to learn about velocity and stuff. But he said no because he didn't know anything about it. We said we would show him how it worked but he just said he was the teacher and we weren't supposed to show him what to do.*
>
> *(Ian, Year 10)*

> *Would Facebook be good to use in class? – Yeah, of course! We use it to help each other with homework. Miss said she didn't want to know, because we aren't allowed to use it in school.*
>
> *(Brianna, Year 9)*

As Ian's comments show, pupils will often be more familiar and significantly more skilled in using newer technology, thus they can often identify learning opportunities that we cannot. Similarly, Brianna's frustrations demonstrate how sometimes the teaching profession can be resistant to change – a barrier to acquiring further technical knowledge (Owen *et al.*, 2006). In the fast-moving world of technology, this can be problematic. Prensky warns that "the single biggest problem facing education today is that our digital immigrant instructors, who speak an outdated language, are struggling to teach a population that speaks an entirely new language" (2001, p. 2). Our pupils have grown up surrounded by new digital technology. Cyber-socialised, they have higher expectations of their digital experiences. It is our role as educators to turn these experiences into learning.

Down in the digital literacy dungeon

So how might popular technology be used in the classroom? To answer this, we have to go back to basics. The new (2013) statutory guidance document for "Computer Programmes of Study" in England stresses the importance of digital literacy to the curriculum. In 2009, the Rose Review had concluded that in order for children to become successful future citizens they would need to be familiar with digital literacy. The argument is fairly straightforward. Modern society has become a digital society, and it is now through our interactions with technology and science that we have come to understand our world. It is therefore essential for everyone to have an understanding, not only about technology itself, but more importantly its impact on our everyday world (Jenkins, 1999). In order to become successful and active members of this digital culture, children need to be equipped with the higher-order skills necessary to be part take in a modern technical society.

A technology and science-based education is therefore seen as being central in preparing all students for lifelong learning. If as educators we need to prepare young people with the necessary digital literacy skills, in order to deal with the challenges of adult life, then our curriculum requires the teaching of appropriate lifelong learning competences so that when young people leave school they can continue to update their technical knowledge by themselves and apply it in their personal and professional lives. Arguably, this approach is most effective when it is grounded in the everyday experiences of young people (Davies, 2005).

But there is a problem. Although ICT and Computing might have an important part to play in a technical society, they are just not very popular in school. Like the sciences, we have seen a steady decline in take up of computer-orientated GCSE and A Level courses and the subsequent reduction in applicants for associated under-graduate courses. This in turn has worried the industry, who see a skill shortage in an area where there was potential to be market leaders. One industry veteran was very clear where the blame lies: "Somehow the classroom got hijacked by ICT. And that is learning about PowerPoint, Word, Excel – useful but boring after more than a week of learning it … we need computer scientists, animators, artists and there aren't enough of them" (Ian Livingstone[1]). Livingstone may indeed have a point, as a group of young people explained to us recently:

> *Here, we have to do ICT up until end of Year 9. It was quite good at first, I hadn't done much at primary school, but it soon got really repetitive. How many PowerPoint presentations do I need to do before I get it? It's not like we can use any of it in our other subjects either. None – except for "Word" of course! But we don't really use much of that either except to submit homework. I mean, there are features (on Word) that we learnt in ICT but I have never touched them again. What's the point then, it's just learning it for the sake of it!*
>
> *(David, Year 11)*

> *It's not interesting! But it could be. We only do it because we have to. I am not doing it as an option, I can do my own thing at home. I have a web site, design cards and things. Don't do none of that in class, Miss won't let us."*
>
> *(Julia, Year 9)*

Julia makes an interesting point. The potential to make computing attractive is often not realised due to poor teaching strategies rather than inadequate resources. She is clearly able to address and develop her computing needs at home, arguably free from the confines of the prescribed curriculum. Like Julia, David is frustrated that what he is being taught is not relevant to his wider technical needs. His comments echo earlier governmental concerns that Science, Technology, Engineering, and Mathematics (STEM) education was becoming increasingly abstracted from the needs and experiences of its participants (Wellcome Trust, 2011).

Compare their comments with the enthusiasm of Vik and Lee from the Science Club:

> *I didn't really like our Science and ICT lessons, but here I saw a different side of it. Like most of us, I play a lot of computer games so Mr Dickens showed us how we could design and program our own levels into the games we liked. It was so different to what we did in class, but I was able to take some of the ideas and use them in my portfolio project.*

> *Vik is right. If ICT was like science club it be sweet, we could do some really interesting stuff if Miss would let us.*

The boys' observations remind us of the importance of teacher enthusiasm in determining engagement. There is evidence from recent research undertaken by the Wellcome Trust (2011) that pupils find STEM an exciting and enjoyable area of study when it is done well. Teachers who acted as a positive influence on attitudes towards learning were reported to be those who made lessons enjoyable, interesting, and understandable through their passion for their subject. As the young people's comments illustrate, engagement with Computing comes down less to *what* is being taught but rather *how* it is actually delivered in the classroom.

Wizards and magic

This is where popular technology has a role to play in the classroom. Take computer games, for example. Perhaps the most popular of the new digital forms, regular game usage in the UK sits at 91 per cent in the 12–15 year age bracket, rising to 94 per cent amongst 8–11 year olds (OFCOM, 2011). Of course, popular usage does not always mean that something is educationally viable, but we believe that there are compelling suggestions as to how they might form the basis of effective pedagogic strategies. Problem solving is a central strand of the digital literacy framework and is usually regarded as a key skill for lifelong learning (Hoskins & Frediksson, 2008). Supporters of computer games argue that digital play can teach users to become effective problem solvers (Crowe & Flynn, 2013). In the best-designed games, players can only advance to a higher level (or unlock better equipment and resources) by "testing out" a range of different approaches and strategies.

Darkstone, the game favoured by Lee, Vik, and Tif at Science Club, works in this way. Players take control of their hero (in Vik's case, his wizard) and manoeuvre him through the fantasy world of Uma, encountering a range of enemies, tasks, and quests set by evil Lord Draak and his minions. As in all good games, things are never simple and many of these encounters become quite complex. Players are required to ask questions such as "What happens if I do this?", "What equipment do I need?" and "Where must I go next?" if they are to overcome the problems set. Successful completion of the game requires lateral thinking and the ability to solve increasingly complex puzzles. As the narrative is a developmental one – it gets harder as the story unfolds – players are required to learn the skills and knowledge they require to solve the next set of challenges. One of the key aspects of the most complex games is that players need to learn to cope with the rigours of the virtual world, thus one of the functions of digital games is that users are being "taught" to "learn". Tif explains further:

> *You start off with basic armour and equipment, but this isn't going to get you very far and you soon have to learn how to make or trade better stuff. Not every weapon or spell will be useful and so you have to learn what to use and when to use it. You remember the last puzzle and try to apply what you have learnt in the next dungeon. It requires a lot of thought. In the quest that Lee is designing here, wizards can only use transformation spells – that's why Vik's character just died, because he couldn't jump the gap. Next time he will hopefully learn what to do. But that is part of the fun.*

Tif touches on one of the fundamental aspects of game-based learning. It offers users the opportunity to experience situated simulations that might not be possible elsewhere. Since it has a well-developed physics engine, *Darkstone*'s gameplay requires that gravity and velocity are just as important as selecting the correct spells or weapon. The young people have to experience and learn how these natural forces impact on different objects in terms of both playing the game and designing their new levels and quests. It is an ongoing and oft-repeated process. The simulated environments of *Darkstone* provide the opportunity to think, understand, prepare, and execute actions.

Computer games facilitate continued practice because negative consequences are not typically associated with failure (Groff *et al.*, 2010).

As Tif points out, in *Darkstone* failure serves as an integral part of the learning experience. Like the best educational experiences, the game is built on logical learning progression or scaffolding. Players are required to learn in an ordered sequence, often directly linked to the immediate challenge that is facing them. Simple skills form the foundation on which more complex knowledge is subsequently based. Yet mastery of skills and knowledge are integral to advancing in the narrative and are often only acquired through repetition and replay.

It is this interactive aspect of digital games that adds to their educational significance, not only because it facilitates informal access to information and knowledge, but also because it is the main cause for its motivational power that makes students feel willing to learn (Leite *et al.*, 2007). Of course, *Darkstone*'s gameplay works because you are drawn into its world – Vik has invested in his wizard character and Lee (as a level designer) in its narrative. As Gee notes, good digital games teach pupils "to solve problems and reflect on the intricacies of the design of imagined worlds and the design of both real and imagined social relationships and identities in the modern world" (2003, p. 48).

Choice and agency

Crystal Island, a science mystery about an epidemic that has struck a team of researchers living on a remote tropical island, offers a further example of how scaffolding is built into a game narrative. Players explore the island, attempting to solve the mystery by interviewing other characters, and using the laboratory equipment (and other resources) to find and examine objects. As the investigation progresses, the player is required to complete an in-game worksheet in order to record results, pose questions, and ultimately offer a diagnosis. The organisation of worksheets provides an opportunity to scaffold the problem-solving process since the game requires a variety of inquiry techniques and there is ample scope to "test out" a range of approaches. Players can talk to sick characters about their symptoms, and consult books and leaflets to try to match what they have been told with known diseases. They can even call upon in-game "experts" to discuss in more depth aspects of different infections. Once they have formulated a hypothesis, they can test this using the virtual research lab to test whether in-game objects have become infected and use the diagnostic worksheet to organise their findings to locate the likely source of the infection.

Both *Darkstone* and *Crystal Island* are important to educational development because they each allow pupils to remain in control of their own learning. This enhances a sense of ownership and agency within the learning process. Lack of agency is a continued criticism of many forms of e-learning and it is significant that digital games have managed to maintain an environment that facilitates both active learning and choice of preferred learning style. This sits in contrast to the closedness of much of the curriculum (Klopfer *et al.*, 2009), as one player explains:

> *It was good to be left to try to figure things out for yourself. I really liked talking to the different characters about their symptoms. Some of them would tell you one thing and others would make how they were feeling sound worse than it was. You have to use the sheet to record things they say. The nurse at the hospital helps you to decide who is telling you the truth.... What did I learn? That different people describe the same symptoms in very different ways. You can't always trust the first thing you are told and you need to look further.*
>
> *(Peter, Year 9)*

Peter highlights an important point, namely the way that digital games promote a multi-faceted approach to problems. Rather than simply resolving a challenge, the student is presented with a whole new level of inquiry. Like the *Darkstone* players, we can see how it is the narrative – in this case, the enigma of how the epidemic is spreading – that facilitates the inquiry process. Of course, the experience is also enjoyable, which motivates Peter to go further, in much the same way that Lee was inspired at the Science Club to create ever more challenging quests. Enjoyment leads to engagement, and pupil engagement is in turn strongly associated with student achievement (Shute *et al.*, 2009). Digital game-based activities have the potential to offer greater levels of engagement than might be found with regular classroom tasks (Rieber, 1996). Of course educators have always employed a variety of methods to keep students interested in the classroom, but for the young people referred to throughout this chapter, it seems to be more than just this. Arguably, it was their affinity with the medium outside of school that sits at the heart of their engagement.

Defending the dark arts

For digital literacy to remain as a key thread of Computing in schools, it needs to extend the application-driven focus of ICT to concentrate on both the digital and the social processes that lie behind technology and how these can be applied to our everyday lives. Computer games – and arguably much popular technology – serve as an interesting platform because, like digital literacy itself, they are seen to address twenty-first century skills (Gee & Shaffer, 2010). The apparent "domesticity" of popular technologies and the features of the digital games themselves afford them a range of advantages, not least in terms of both learning skills and education environment. In this respect, popular technologies should not only be seen as tools for learning but as "sites" where many kinds of social practices can be played out for pedagogical benefit (Goodfellow & Lea, 2007).

Digital games have traditionally been caught in a tension between narratology (games as "stories") and ludology (games as formal rule-based systems or "simulations"). As we saw in *Darkstone*, digital games allow users to extend their gameplay by modifying and developing aspects of the game environment. In the case of the Science Club trio, this acts as an extension to their learning around computer science. But for other students, it helps facilitate an insight into the ways that digital simulations are constructed. But it would be wrong to dismiss digital games as simple simulations of the "real world". Parker (2004) suggests that the "realism" of games lies not just in the ability to simulate the material world as an aesthetic, but in its accurate re-creation of material social processes as well.

Of course, games are just one of many strategies that can be deployed, and whilst popularity on its own is not a precursor to educational attainment, we have tried to argue that digital games have a role to play in the classroom – perhaps not as an alternative to more traditional modes of teaching, but certainly as a pedagogic tool to complement them. The importance of digital games to digital literacy lies in their ability to address a wide spectrum of learning styles within a complex decision-making framework (Squire, 2005). Students are required to think systematically and take a relational approach rather than rely on isolated facts or ideas. The complexity of a gaming environment directs students not just to apply knowledge but more importantly to adapt it to changing scenarios. This is arguably what we saw in the Science Club at the start of this chapter, and what we as teachers should be striving for in our classrooms.

Note

1. www.bbc.co.uk/news/technology-15240207.

References

BECTA (2009) "Harnessing Technology Review 2009: The role of technology in education and skills". [Online]. Available at: http://dera.ioe.ac.uk/1422/1/becta_2009_htreview_report.pdf (accessed 15 December 2013).

Byron. T. (2010) "Do we have safer children in a digital world? A review of progress since the 2008 Byron Review". [Online]. Available at: http://webarchive.nationalarchives.gov.uk/20130401151715/https://www.education.gov.uk/publications/eOrderingDownload/DCSF-00290-2010.pdf (accessed 11 April 2014).

Coran-Jones, R (2011) *Can the UK Raise its Game?* Available at www.bbc.co.uk/news/technology-15240207.

Crowe, N. (2013) "Online gaming and digital fantasy for scientific literacy". In D.M. Watts (ed.) *Debates in Science Education*, London: Routledge.

Crowe, N., & Flynn, S. (2013) "Hunting down the monster: Using multi-play digital games and on-line virtual worlds in secondary school teaching". In M. Leask (ed.) *Learning to Teach Using ICT in the Secondary School* (3rd edn), Abingdon: Routledge/Taylor Francis.

Davies, B. (2005) "Youth work: A manifesto for our times", *Youth and Policy*, 88(1): 23. Leicester: National Youth Agency.

Department for Education and Skills (2003) "Towards a Unified e-Learning Strategy". [Online]. Available at: www.education.gov.uk/consultations/downloadableDocs/towards%20a%20unified%20e-learning%20strategy.pdf (accessed 4 December 2013).

Freire, P. (1985) *The Politics of Education*, Massachusetts: Bergin & Garvey Publishers.

Gee, J.P. (2003) *What Video Games Have to Teach Us About Learning and Literacy*, New York: Palgrave Macmillan.

Gee, J.P. (2007) *Good Video Games and Good Learning: Collected Essays on Video Games, Learning, and Literacy*, New York: Peter Lang.

Gee, J.P., & Shaffer, D.W. (2010) "Looking where the light is bad: Video games and the future of assessment" (Epistemic Games Group Working Paper No. 2010–02), Madison: University of Wisconsin-Madison. Retrieved from http://epistemicgames.org/eg/looking-where-the-light-is-bad (downloaded 15 March 2012).

Goodfellow, R., & Lea, M. (2007) *Challenging E-Learning in the University: A Literacies Perspective*, Society for Research into Higher Education, Maidenhead: McGraw Hill/Open University Press.

Greenwald, S., & Rosner, D. (2003) "Are we distance educating our students to death? Some reflections on the educational assumptions of distance learning", *Radical Pedagogy*, 2003.

Groff, J., Howells, C., & Cranmer, S. (2010). *The Impact of Console Games in the Classroom: Evidence from Schools in Scotland*, UK: Futurelab.

Hoskins, B., & Fredriksson, U. (2008) *Learning to Learn: What Is It and Can It Be Measured?* JRC, European Commission Document.

Jenkins, E.W. (1999) "School science, citizenship and the public understanding of science", *International Journal of Science Education*, 21: 703–710.

Klopfer, E., Osterweil, S., Groff, J., & Haas, J. (2009) *Using the Technology of Today, in the Classroom Today: The Instructional Power of Digital Games, Social Networking, Simulations and How Teachers Can Leverage Them.* [Online]. Available at: http://education.mit.edu/papers/GamesSimsSocNets_EdArcade.pdf (accessed 3 January 2014).

Leask, M. (2001) *Issues in Teaching Using ICT*, London: RoutledgeFalmer.

Leite, L., Vieira, P., Silva, R., & Neves, T. (2007) "The role of WebQuests in science education for citizenship", *Interactive Educational Multimedia*, 15: 18–36.

Livingstone, S. (2012) "Critical reflections on the benefits of ICT in education", *Oxford Review of Education*, 38(1): 9–24.

McAlister, Andrea (2009, August–September). "Teaching the Millennial Generation", *American Music Teacher*, 13–15.

OFCOM (2011) *Children and Parents: Media Use and Attitudes Report*. Available at http://stakeholders.ofcom.org.uk/binaries/research/media-literacy/oct2011/Children_and_parents.pdf (downloaded 14 November 2012).

Owen, M., Grant, L., Sayers, S., & Facer, K. (2006) "Social software and learning", *Futurelab*. [Online]. Available at: http://www2.futurelab.org.uk/resources/documents/opening_education/Social_Software_report.pdf (accessed 3 January 2014).

Parker, K. (2004) "Free play: The politics of the video game", *Reason Online*, www.reason.com/0404/fe.kp.free.shtml (downloaded 6 June 2010).

Postman, N. (1985) *Amusing Ourselves to Death: Public Discourse in the Age of Show Business*, London: Heinemann.

Prensky, M. (2001) "Digital natives, digital immigrants", *On the Horizon*, MCB University Press, 9 (5 October).

Rieber, L.P. (1996) "Seriously considering play: Designing interactive learning environments based on the blending of microworlds, simulations, and games", *Educational Technology Research & Development*, 44(2): 43–58.

Rose, J. (2009) *Independent Review of the Primary Curriculum: Final Report*. [Online]. Available at: www.educationengland.org.uk/documents/pdfs/2009-IRPC-final-report.pdf (accessed 17 November 2013).

Shute, V.J., Ventura, M., Bauer, M.I., & Zapata-Rivera, D. (2009). "Melding the power of serious games and embedded assessment to monitor and foster learning: Flow and grow". In U. Ritterfeld, M. Cody, & P. Vorderer (eds) *Serious Games: Mechanisms and Effects*, Mahwah, NJ: Routledge, Taylor and Francis.

Simpson, D., Todd, I., & Toyn, M. (2011) "ICT as a core skill". In D. Simpson & M. Toyn (eds) *Primary ICT Across the Curriculum*, Exeter: Learning Matters.

Squire, K. (2005) "Changing the game: What happens when video games enter the classroom?", *Innovate; Online Journal of Education*, August/September, www.innovateonline.info (downloaded 14 September 2005).

Underwood, J. (2009) "The impact of digital technology: A review of the evidence of the impact of digital technologies on formal education". *BECTA*. [Online]. Available at: www.ictliteracy.info/rf.pdf/impact-digital-tech.pdf (accessed 17 November 2013).

Valentine, G., Marsh, J., & Pattie, C. (2005) "Children and young people's home use of ICT for educational purposes: The impact on attainment at Key Stages 1–4". [Online]. Available at: http://webarchive.nationalarchives.gov.uk/2013040 1151715/https://www.education.gov.uk/publications/eOrderingDownload/ RR672.pdf (accessed 29 November 2013).

Wellcome Trust (2011) *Exploring Young People's Views of Science Education*, London: Wellcome Trust.

Wellington, J. (2005) "Has ICT come of age? Recurring debates on the role of ICT in education, 1982–2004", *Research in Science & Technological Education*, 23(1): 25–39.

Glossary

algorithm a set of instructions that is given to a computer to direct it to complete a specific task. This idea can be introduced to younger pupils by describing a simple parallel with other sets of instructions, such as baking a cake: if the instructions are incomplete or contain flaws, you don't end up with a cake! Accuracy is vital.

bit the basic unit of information in computing and digital communications. It has a single numerical value, either "1" or "0", which encodes a single unit of digital information.

Boolean logic named after the nineteenth-century mathematician George Boole, Boolean logic is a form of algebra in which all values are reduced to being either TRUE or FALSE. Boolean logic is especially important for computer science because it fits neatly with the binary numbering system, in which each bit has a value of either 1 or 0. Another way of looking at it is that each bit can only be either TRUE or FALSE. See also "bit" above.

browser the program that you use to access the *internet* and view web pages on your computer. It has been likened to the "key to the door" of the internet.

client a piece of computer hardware or software that accesses a service made available by a server. It is therefore like the person who actually visits the library.

code, or coding   a systematic collection of rules, which instruct a computer to work. Coding in Scratch is a visual form of coding. It is also called block coding, as the code is clicked, dragged, and assembled in blocks. Coding in Python is a text-based form. At KS3, both types of coding are a requirement. Logo is called a graphic programming language.

computer networks   a series of computers connected together by wires and terminals, often connected also to the internet. They allow people to share information. A school network allows easy storage and organisation of pupils' work, as well as potentially being an internal "library" of digital information.

control   instructions that tell the computer to change "physical systems", such as making a robot move. An example would be using Logo to move a turtle around the floor in prescribed ways.

data   facts and statistics collected together for reference or analysis. They represent such things as digitised text, images, sound, or video files, which can be processed or transmitted by a computer.

debug   to identify and correct errors in a computer program. This can easily be achieved using Scratch, as pupils will want to make a Sprite move in a particular way, and will want to debug their program in order to make this happen according to their wishes, and their imagination.

digital artefacts   materials made by using a computer (this term also refers to errors made to data).

digital content   any data created, edited, stored, or viewed on a computer, such as text, images, sound, and video. When these elements are combined, it is called "multi-media".

digital literacy   a general term, meaning the understanding of computers and how they work. It applies to the last sections on the Programmes of Study, such as the ability to "recognise common uses of ICT beyond school".

e-safety   a set of guidelines designed to keep pupils safe when using computers, especially when using the internet. This is usually set out in a School Policy, and includes information about what to do, and whom to contact, if pupils find inappropriate or disturbing material.

hypertext   text displayed on a computer or other electronic device, with references (called "hyperlinks") to other text that the reader can immediately access, usually by a mouse click, key press sequence, or by touching the screen. It is text that tells the computer to do something, and so is "hyper" (over or beyond) text.

information knowledge derived from data (raw facts and statistics). This means that data has to be processed, in order to give it meaning. It involves understanding the data, and constructing knowledge from it.

input data provided to a computer system, such as through a keyboard, a mouse, a microphone, a camera, or sensors (e.g. heat or light sensors).

internet the interconnected system of computer networks, all using a shared protocol: TCP – a protocol or code developed for the internet to get data from one network device to another, and IP – a code used to label packets of data sent across the internet, identifying both the sending and the receiving computers in order to communicate.

logical reasoning a systematic approach to solving problems, or deducing information using a set of reliable rules. In the classroom, careful questioning of pupils about changes to their coding might be: "What do you think will happen next?" and "Why do you think this?" This is one way forward. Some schools have "thinking skills" as part of their curriculum, and start with an advantage...

output the information produced by a computer system for its user, typically on a screen, through speakers or on a printer, but also through the control of robots.

packets of data a packet is a formatted unit of data; a "chunk" of information.

physical systems linked items of hardware, like a robot turtle, or a heat measuring system, controlled by a computer.

program a stored set of instructions in a language that is understood by the computer, and that does some form of computation.

Python a computer programming language that is text-based. It is usually introduced at secondary level (KS3 and KS4).

repetition a programming construct in which one or more instructions are repeated, perhaps a certain number of times, until a condition is satisfied, or until the program is stopped.

robot a machine or device that operates automatically, or by remote control.

Scratch a visual programming language, developed at MIT. The best version for pupils is 1.4 as it is easy to use in the early stages of a project. Version 2.00 is more powerful and more sophisticated, and therefore makes a good "second step" for pupils. Start with version 1.4. It uses block coding, that is clicking and dragging, and assembling instructions using blocks of code from the options in the program, such as Control, Motion, and Sound.

search   to find data, for example on the internet. Pupils need to learn to understand and identify data that satisfies one or more search conditions, such as web pages containing certain keywords.

search engine   a computer program that searches for, and identifies, items in a database that correspond to keywords specified by the user, used especially for finding particular sites on the internet.

selection   a set of instructions determined by whether a particular condition is met.

sequence (as a verb)   to place programming code in order, with each element executed one after the other.

server   a computer that responds to requests across a computer network to provide a service. In this respect, it is similar to a library, where people ask for books to borrow, and are served by a librarian.

services   programs, usually on the internet, which respond to requests. These include such services as transmitting a web page, sending and receiving emails, or video-conferencing, such as Skype.

simulations   imitations of the operation of a real-world process or system over time. The act of simulating something first requires that a computer model is developed. They are an important part of computer games.

software   software is a general term. It can refer to all computer instructions in general, or to any specific set of computer instructions, such as web browsers and computer games. It also now includes "apps" (applications) for mobile phones.

URL   Uniform Resource Locator – the address of a web site.

variables   a symbolic name associated with a value, and whose value may be changed. They are used to store, retrieve, or change simple data. Variables report a value, store a value, or change a value. These are used, for example, in creating user scores in a computer game.

Venn diagram   a diagram that represents mathematical or logical sets in a pictorial form, such as by circles, or closed curves within an enclosing rectangle.

VOIP   Voice Over Internet Protocol. Used, for example, for making telephone calls over the internet.

World Wide Web   a system of interlinked hypertext documents, accessed via the internet. These pages can be transmitted to users through web servers, such as Google and Yahoo.

Index

Page numbers in *italics* denote tables, those in **bold** denote figures.